STYLE AND PLANNING

GENERAL EDITOR: CAROLINE BOISSET

STYLE AND PLANNING

STEPHEN ANDERTON AND NIGEL COLBORN

PRACTICAL AND INSPIRATIONAL ADVICE
ON PLANNING YOUR IDEAL GARDEN

MITCHELL BEAZLEY

THE GARDEN DESIGNER STYLE AND PLANNING

First published by Mitchell Beazley in 1993 as
The Garden Sourcebook

Mitchell Beazley
An imprint of Reed Consumer Books Limited
Michelin House
81 Fulham Road
London SW3 6RB

Editors Emily Wright, Simon Ryder,
    David Joyce, Richard Rosenfeld
Designers Jeremy Roots, Geoff Fennell
Senior Art Editors Larraine Lacey, Mike Brown
Editorial Assistant Jaspal Bhangra
Production Controller Sarah Schuman
Commissioned Photography Sue Atkinson,
    Paul Barker
Commissioned Artwork Tony Graham, Andrew
    Macdonald, Coral Mula, Gillie Newman, Sandra
    Pond, Will Giles
Picture Research Christine Rista
Executive Editor Sarah Polden
Design Director Jacqui Small

The six gardens shown on pages 24-29 were
designed by Alison Coleman and illustrated by
Vivien Monument.

A CIP catalogue record for this book is available
from the British Library

ISBN 1 8573 2486 2

The publishers have made every effort to ensure
that all instructions given in this book are accurate
and safe, but they cannot accept liability for any
resulting injury, damage or loss to either person or
property whether direct or consequential and
howsoever arising. The authors and publishers will
be grateful for any information which will assist
them in keeping future editions up to date.

Typeset in Plantin by SX Composing Ltd,
Rayleigh, Essex
Colour reproduction by Mandarin Offset,
Hong Kong
Produced by Mandarin Offset, Hong Kong
Printed and bound in Hong Kong

Contents

FIRST
STEPS

FIRST STEPS

Anyone can have a dream garden. No matter where you live, or how undeveloped your horticultural skills, creating the perfect garden is not only feasible, but much easier than you might think. Few are lucky enough to inherit an ideal site but hardly anyone finds a truly hopeless situation. The art of gardening is evaluating what you have got and transforming it into what you want. And above all knowing exactly how to do it. One simply cannot visit enough different specialist gardens to see the full range of available effects. Investigate the formal Renaissance style, cottage garden informality (or even chaos), Mediterranean courtyards, one-colour borders, water features and gardens with inventive examples of topiary. On seeing something you like, note down how the effect is achieved. As a vital complement to these records, keep enormous lists of plants.

All good gardeners cheat. The more you borrow ideas the better. If it works recreate it. If you cannot provide exactly the same growing conditions then play around with the idea and reinvent it: amend it to your own needs. If you like formal gardens then the range of tricks is huge; more or less everything can be whipped into art. Hedges can be given windows onto contrasting areas, with "doors" leading into corridors and alleys. Never settle for the obvious.

You have to be equally imaginative with plants. When you find a particular plant that you like the next step is to visit a national collection. Most countries have them. See if there is a variety with even better colour, scent, or both. Also get into the habit of visiting major horticultural shows. Thereafter start visiting small specialist nurseries which invariably sell a wider range of rare plants than garden centres.

While at times one relishes getting carried away, beware of totally overdoing it. Creating a garden is one thing, time-consuming and expensive though it can be. But looking after it year after year is something else. Shrubs are a godsend if only because they tend to require relatively little attention. One of the biggest pitfalls is collecting tender perennials: because so many are exotic, they need to be kept in pots in a frost-free greenhouse over winter, or indoors. It is easy to run out of space and money for fresh compost and eventually even bigger containers.

But given some basic knowledge, a clear idea of the do's and don'ts, and three key ingredients – time, patience and the will to make it work, then everything will go according to plan. Your dream garden can become a reality. And sooner rather than later.

ASSESSING THE SITE
Whether the site is brand new or an old established plot, the same principles apply to planning and designing your ideal garden. First, assess what is at your disposal, then decide what kind of garden you want and whether you can provide its requirements. For example, a kitchen garden needs fertile soil and full sun, whereas woodland species need shade; alpine and rock plants need less space than an arboretum, when nothing less than about 4 acres (1.6 hectares) will do justice to a collection.

For most purposes, one needs reasonably fertile soil and a sunny, sheltered position, but even without these ingredients do not give up. Assess your garden's potential, its strengths and weaknesses, and then decide how to take advantage of the former while minimizing the effects of the latter. It is the surest way to successful garden design.

Dimensions
The first step with a new garden is to familiarize yourself with its dimensions. Size matters, but only in so far as it might limit the number of different areas you can create, and the size and number of plants and features within them.

If the garden is on the small side, there are several ways of putting the available space to more efficient use. Vertical surfaces, for instance, offer scope for climbers, wall plants and hanging baskets. The range of plants is enormous. One small area could contain the dark red flowers of *Clematis viticella* growing up through the long catkin-like racemes of *Itea ilicifolia*, with a *Cytisus battandieri* nearby bearing early summer, pineapple-scented, yellow flowers. Though the latter is strictly speaking a freestanding tree, it can also be grown against a sunny wall. Raised beds and terraces also extend the growing areas, and containers make maximum use of sterile locations such as paving and window sills.

Furthermore, the *illusion* of size is easily achieved. Clever design demonstrates how even the most cramped plots can, with crafty positioning of screens in the form of hedges and trellises, give a spurious impression of size and stature. The secret is to have a surprise around every corner, and to make the visitor think there are more corners than really exist. One of the most sophisticated forms of illusion is *trompe l'oeil*. At its most developed, it involves painting a scene on a wall of an extra area beyond, but receding trelliswork and the clever use of mirrors can easily give an impression of depth that does not exist.

Incidentally, too large a garden can also cause problems, although they are easily solved by strategic planting, with the emphasis on trees and shrubs underplanted with ground cover. However, since the great majority of gardeners find themselves with limited space rather than too much, this text will concentrate on that extreme rather than coping with extensive acres. By itself smallness is not a problem, what counts is how it is used.

Planning considerations
When planning your garden, once you have accepted the size of the site, begin by considering these four factors: shape, topography, division and ambience.
Shape This influences design considerably. Few plots are symmetrical but that really does not matter. Indeed, an L-shape or a triangle offers more design potential than a rectangle. Perhaps the most difficult shape of all is a square, particularly when it is too

small to subdivide, but even this problem has solutions (see pages 26 and 27).

Topography Surprisingly, a level site is less desirable than one with interesting, gradual changes, and the attraction of a slope is that it often provides the possibility of terracing. Since steep slopes are unstable, especially when cultivated, devices such as retaining walls, steps or buttresses are needed.

Division Hedges, walls and fences make ideal screens and can introduce different moods and styles as you walk through the garden. They are also invaluable for screening off unsightly but essential areas like the compost heap and refuse storage areas, but do not just erect screens and then forget about them. They ought to be attractive, architectural features. Hedges, for example, in addition to decorative entrances and exits, can be given scalloped or battlemented tops. Alternatively, you could plant a tapestry hedge consisting of hornbeam and *Lonicera nitida*.

A design for an awkward garden shape needs to be carefully thought out. A long thin area, for example, can be divided into contrasting sections (the Mediterranean garden, the black and white garden, the ornamental kitchen garden) by means of barriers across its width, but by leaving a narrow view running through from end to end you create an additional vista.

Above: By emphasising the rectangular shape of this area with a double border, paths and a narrow lawn, the eye is drawn towards the wrought iron gates at the end.

Below: Sloping ground can be landscaped with borders running across the incline. The effect of this is informal and relaxing, whereas terracing is more formal.

Furthermore, by placing an ornamental feature for example, a statue, seat or urn at the far end, you gain the full benefit from the sites length while the screens minimize the disadvantages.

Ambience The atmosphere of a potential garden is an important consideration. Even when you are working on a bare site the potential of the space needs to be

assessed and compared with the "feel" you want to achieve. Walk around the area, take measurements, and observe natural features such as wet spots, bumps or edges, and any other quirks and oddities because they may well have the potential to become focal points. The emphasis is on making use of your natural resources and converting the apparently insignificant into eye-catching attractions.

CLIMATE AND MICROCLIMATE
Geographical location
Climate is all-important because it dictates the kinds of plants you can grow and exerts an immense influence on design. If you have moved to a new area it is easy to discover average temperatures and rainfall, but you must always allow for extremes.

Regional climate is influenced by fundamental geographical factors like latitude, altitude, proximity of large land masses and the sea and the influence of major ocean currents. Every district has its own special quirks too, such as the Mistral, a cold wind funnelled down the Rhône Valley in France, the "Fremantle Doctor", a cooling wind that relieves the inhabitants of Perth in Western Australia from heatwaves, and the high altitude of the Alps and Rockies that shortens the growing season.

Below: Coastal gardens often have many different microclimates which are quite distinct from the surrounding area. Accordingly, an astounding range of tender plants can be grown on the more sheltered sites.

Above: Besides forming boundaries, walls and hedges provide essential shelter, improving the climate within the garden. When picking building materials or hedging plants, make sure they match the planting.

Then there are microclimates, natural and artificial. For example, in most winters central London is nearly frost-free because of the artificial heat exuded by the city. Consequently many tender plants like certain abutilons can be kept outside while in colder country areas they have to be tucked up in a conservatory over winter. More surprisingly, given the northerly latitude, gardens on the northwest coast of Scotland can grow subtropical plants outdoors with minimal risk of damage because of the moderating effect of the Gulf Stream. In the Pacific Northwest of the United States the climate is made more temperate and wetter than adjacent regions by warm Pacific currents, giving milder winters than are found in the more southerly Kansas.

Though it is wise to learn about your local climate, it is equally important to set about creating your own special microclimate. You cannot do much about the weather but you can do a great deal to minimize its effects, perhaps by erecting a protective windbreak against slicing, icy winds. Often, famous established gardens succeed because their creators have taken great care to improve conditions, enabling them to grow a wider range of delicate and more interesting plants. In cold areas frost and snow do no harm provided you are growing hardy plants and no tender perennials have been left outside. A much bigger problem is wind. It dehydrates soil and stunts growth, while constant buffeting bruises young emerging plant tissue, impairing growth. The first task, therefore, in trying to influence the climate in a new garden is to eliminate or at least reduce the potentially destructive wind.

Creating shelter

If the site is badly exposed, conditions may be too unpleasant for even shelter plants to establish themselves, in which case you will need to erect either temporary or permanent windbreaks. Although it may seem like a good idea to build a solid wall, this does more harm than good. The wind will eddy over the top of the wall and swirl down, creating a whirlwind effect in the garden. The only solution is to create a filtering windbreak that is approximately 40 percent porous, which significantly reduces wind speed and impact but does not stop it dead. Since the screen should become an attractive garden feature in its own right rather than a simply functional object, plants are preferable to fencing, but they do, of course, take longer to develop.

Windbreaks usually protect an area ten times their height, so they will produce an immediate change to the growing conditions within the enclosure. For example, two of them running from east to west on either side of a garden will create a dark, cool side and a warm, well-lit one. The advantage of such a windbreak is that it provides an opportunity for two contrasting garden areas, each with its own range of plants, each with its own character.

The type of screen chosen depends on personal preference. Walls will need to have trees or shrubs planted nearby to minimize the eddying effect of the wind; evergreens or matching shrubs successfully complement such solid structures. Alternatively, consider hedges, whether clipped formally or kept in trim with an annual haircut. For a more natural look, thickly planted shrubs, interspersed with taller trees, create a good shelter belt. The selection of plants should ensure a changing pattern of interest running through the seasons with spring blossom, fresh, exciting, contrasting foliage in summer, autumn berries and interesting twigs, branches and bark over winter. Pay particular attention to colour, texture and outline. With thoughtful planning you will be able to

Below: Although a frost-covered border is an attractive sight, especially on sunny days, vulnerable plants may not survive unless protected. However, those plants growing near house walls are less likely to suffer from frost damage.

Right: As a general rule, rather than fight against the soil type of your garden, select plants to suit the prevailing conditions. Without a naturally peaty, acid soil, this striking planting of colourful azaleas would not be possible.

create an outstanding garden feature which is also functional. This does not have to be formal and symmetrical; a seemingly random planting will blur the garden boundary and give the illusion of space.

Frost

Frost in winter is seldom a problem unless you want to grow bananas outdoors in upstate New York or daturas on the Cotswold hills. Given that there are in excess of 60,000 hardy plants to choose from, even the coldest areas can be successfully planted up to suit most tastes.

Frost at the wrong time of year, on the other hand, is disastrous. It kills tender young growth, destroys spring blossom and, in extreme cases, wipes out whole plants, especially the marginally hardy. The most likely scenario for unseasonal frost is a clear, still night which follows a calm, bright day. Without wind currents to move it, cold air accumulates in low places, like water forming a pool at the lowest level. The problem with erecting shelter is that it increases the danger of untimely frost by damming up cold air. This is particularly likely on a hillside or in a hollow and is called a frost pocket. A natural frost pocket cannot be eliminated, but you can at least reduce the problem by creating perimeter gaps so that the cold air flows out of the garden and away.

Having said that, though, it is worth stressing that winter frost can be a fantastic advantage. This is particularly true of gardens strong on structure, with topiary or with clipped low hedges roping in different areas. Not only can the form of plants be more clearly appreciated than in summer when they are usually part-hidden by flowers, but such architectural shapes look quite sensational when crested with frost. The same goes for plants in the herbaceous border. Many gardeners cut down the straggly growth in autumn, but this can easily be left until the following spring so that it, too, will give a fine display of crisp, frosty, mid-winter outlines.

SOIL TYPES

How inappropriate and demeaning that, in certain parts of the English-speaking world, soil is known as dirt. First-rate gardens cannot exist without excellent soil. If yours is poor and infertile then it has to be improved. Drastic steps may be necessary, but first, since soils vary hugely in texture, structure and quality, it is vital that you begin by assessing its character. The soil in any area is the product of local geology. During the ice ages glaciation transported huge quantities of rock across the globe. Each type of rock responded differently to weathering so that limestone bedrock, for example, broke down to a very different material than volcanic rock. Some areas, such as the Rhine Valley in Germany, benefit from loess, a fine, fertile soil formed by wind erosion. However, the most fertile soils are found in flood plains, being the sediment deposited by rivers.

Soil is a living material. If healthy it contains billions of micro-organisms that live off the organic content which mainly consists of decaying vegetation. Good soil must also contain moisture and oxygen, and usually carries a high proportion of mineral particles. When very fine, the soil resembles clay; when coarse, a sandy loam. On fenland and peatland the topsoil may be composed almost entirely of organic material, the result of millennia of sedges or mosses living and dying, gradually building up and forming a thick layer of fibrous material.

Most gardeners need only know whether their soil is clay-like or sandy. Clay retains moisture, is difficult to work and sticky when wet, and sets very hard with surface cracks in a dry summer. It needs regular breaking up over winter with a soil conditionier (for example, mushroom compost), although it is often very fertile in its own right. Sandy soil is easy to work and dries out quickly, but needs plenty of well-rotted manure or compost to improve moisture retention. Alluvial silt in a flood plain is an exception to the sandy rule; it is easy to work, fertile and, though free-draining, excellent at retaining moisture.

Acidity and Alkalinity

Plants manufacture their own food by converting carbon dioxide in the atmosphere into carbohydrates. Other essential ingredients come from mineral salts dissolved in the water that coats the soil particles. Nitrogen, phosphorus and potassium are needed in fairly large quantities, with minor but vital additions of magnesium, calcium, sulphur, oxygen, iron, manganese, boron, molybdenum, copper and zinc.

Plants differ in their ability to take up these mineral nutrients. Some are only efficient at absorbing iron, for example, in acid soil, while others can obtain everything they need in the most alkaline conditions. That is why it is essential to know the character of your soil. If it is alkaline you will not be able to grow lime-haters such as rhododendrons or camellias. In very acid soils limestone plants such as philadelphus, clematis and dianthus will flounder. You can easily buy cheap pH testing kits which you should apply to different parts of the garden since conditions will vary. (The pH refers to the negative decimal logarithm of hydrogen ion concentration expressed in moles per litre.) A pH of 7 is neutral; anything higher (and the scale goes up to 14) is alkaline, and anything

Left: To achieve this kind of display year after year, the soil must be kept in good order, with regular additions of bulky organic matter and appropriate feeding.

Right: In a very informal setting aim for naturalistic planting. This woodland scene includes groups of various shade-tolerant plants such as hostas.

lower is acid. Generally, most plants thrive at 6.4-7, vegetables preferring 7-7.5. To confirm your readings look around the neighbourhood to see what plants are growing well in other people's gardens. If you want to increase soil alkalinity add lime. But note: such a step tends to be irrevocable so think carefully before you act. It is not so easy to increase the acidity. The best way is to create raised beds filled with acid soil.

Improving the soil

There are a number of ways to improve the quality of the soil; drainage can be made more efficient and the substance and fertility of the soil enhanced.

Drainage The most important consideration on any land that is to be productive is drainage. This fact has been recognized almost as long as gardening has been a practice. The ancient Roman poet Virgil, a keen horticulturist, waxed lyrical about it. While soil must contain water if it is to sustain plant growth, saturation or waterlogging can be as harmful as drying out. This can be fatal. If water fills all the interstices between the soil particles there is no room for air, and so the essential oxygen, and the plant roots begin to rot. Good drainage enables water to pass through the soil and run away to its natural level. In well-drained soils, root development is unimpeded and roots will grow to surprising depths, improving the plants efficiency at absorbing nutrients and therefore maximizing growth and vigour.

Some soils drain naturally, but not all can be relied upon to do so. In a particularly damp garden it may be worth considering installing a drainage system. The most effective consist of underground pipes laid in trenches at regular intervals and backfilled with gravel, but this is an expensive procedure. Cheaper but less effective methods include digging organic material or sand and gravel into the soil. Such measures may not assist deep drainage, but they do improve soil condition just below the surface. Raising borders slightly to produce a trench along their edges also improves drainage, particularly for shallow-rooted plants. Some species are slightly more tolerant of wet feet than others, but there is still no substitute for truly efficient, beneficial drainage.

Building up the soil Soil that has been well managed will be rich in organic matter and therefore rich in beneficial micro-organisms. If you are lucky enough to inherit a garden in good condition then rejoice, but remember you have got to keep working at it. If the soil is poor do not despair, but start digging in whatever rotted or rotting vegetation you can find manure,

leaf mould, compost, and so on. Thereafter, treat your soil as a hungry beast and feed it with compost or manure every year. After three summers you should notice a considerable difference.

Fertility To thrive, plants need adequate levels of every essential plant nutrient, but in the act of gardening you automatically remove vital plant material, such as crops and prunings, so these lost minerals need replacing. Furthermore, many garden plants have been bred to grow faster and larger than their wild counterparts so need higher levels of nutrients.

Manure used as a soil conditioner also tackles this problem, but it is not always available. Fortunately plant foods are easy to come by, either organic (such as fish or bone meal) or inorganic (in the form of proprietary products). The concentration of nutrients in inorganic fertilizers varies, the exact ratio sometimes being indicated by the letters NPK. The accompanying numbers, say 10:11:27, indicate a ratio of 10 percent nitrogen, 11 percent phosphorus and 27 percent potassium. Nitrogen promotes leaf growth, phosphorus ripens fruit and potassium produces good fruit and flowers. Generally, a balanced, all-in-one fertilizer is adequate, but sometimes a plant needs extra quantities of one nutrient. For example, leafy vegetables like spinach need heavy nitrogen application.

High fertility, once achieved, needs to be kept at that level. I use dried poultry waste at roughly a double handful per square yard (square metre) once a year on my mixed borders. This works well as a source of nitrogen, phosphorus and potassium. (Occasionally, I have missed a year but the garden has not suffered because the general level of fertility in the soil is high.)

Soil structure and damage

Inexperienced gardeners often fail to recognize the fragility of soil structure. While some soils are less stable than others, all are liable to damage. The main problem is compaction. This results from mechanical pressure which forces the particles together, driving out the air and spoiling the environment for micro-organisms. In extreme cases roots will be unable to penetrate and water will not drain away. Light, sandy soils may not suffer, but heavier soils with a high clay content can be ruined and are particularly prone to compaction if walked on when wet. It is like stepping on, and sinking into, semi-hard concrete, and does plant roots no good whatsoever. The best way to avoid this problem involves creating beds never more than one footstep wide with stone paths running between, so there is no need to walk on the soil. The ideal is rarely practical in the flower garden, but you can minimize difficulties when doing winter projects by laying planks on the soil surface. These reduce the pressure on the ground, distributing weight more evenly, and are better to tread on than mud.

A hard compacted layer below the surface is known as a "pan". It can be created by the weight of a mechanical cultivator, although you may not be aware of the problem because the surface soil can still look friable or crumbly. One of the worst instances occurs when a garden has previously been used as a building site. The contractors will have churned up the subsoil and afterwards, as a cosmetic exercise, spread a load or two of imported topsoil over the plot. Standing water after rain is a sure sign, but even without it, investigate the state of the soil sooner rather than later.

Once the pan forms it impedes drainage and needs to be broken up. Various tools are available, those particularly worth considering being mechanical cultivators which have an extension at the back designed to crack through the pan as the machine drives forward. Otherwise, compaction is best repaired by deep digging and by incorporating bulky material, particularly in heavy soils, to open up the structure and let in oxygen. In cold areas, deep digging can be done in autumn and the ground left rough during winter, allowing the action of frost and thawing to convert clotted land into a more manageable tilth.

To conclude this section, three examples of problem soils are given with suggested treatments.

Heavy, sticky clay The problem with clay is that it does not forgive abuse, being easily damaged and difficult to repair. Any means of making it more porous and getting more air into the mix will improve growing conditions. The prime objective is to build up the humus by digging in bulky compost. As the garden develops, be assiduous in your composting, hoarding every scrap of organic refuse from rose prunings to

kitchen waste. Farmyard manure, if you can obtain it, is beneficial, adding humus as well as nutrients. Further additions of coarse grit, shingle and even ash will also open up the texture and give a crumbly, more manageable texture in which plants thrive.

In many respects the plants themselves help to improve heavy soils. The roots penetrate and open the structure, while falling foliage increases the organic content so that gradually, over the years, the surface soil becomes easier to work.

To establish new plants in the heaviest soils you must improve conditions around their roots. When digging planting holes incorporate extra quantities of leaf mould enriched with bone meal or a slow release fertilizer at the bottom to ensure rapid establishment. The one huge compensation for having heavy clay is that once the plants have settled they succeed much better than in less fertile ground.

Fine, blowing sand In some areas, particularly near the coast, shifting sands or sandy soil may cause problems. Unlike clay which stays put, sand at its worst can literally blow away, leaving roots exposed, or it can blow in, depositing a desert-like dune over the entire surface of the garden.

The main advantage of sandy soil is that it is easy to work and difficult to damage. The drawback is that water runs straight through it, flushing away dissolved mineral salts, leaving plants dry and undernourished. It may seem contradictory to suggest that organic matter is the best way of adding body when it also lightens heavy clay, but it does work. The addition of humus in the form of leaf mould or rotted manure improves moisture retention. In the case of

Below left: Shade makes for special planting opportunities. Glossy evergreen foliage is always useful, while pale variegated leaves can be used to highlight areas.

Right: The area next to a wall will be shaded and dry because of the rain shadow cast by the wall. The self-clinging *Hydrangea petiolaris* is a good choice for such a site.

existing beds which need bulking up, it may be necessary to remove all the plants, transferring them to a temporary bed, while the soil is being treated. Most sands tend to be acid, so if you want to grow food, mix lime into the soil.

Thin topsoil over chalk or bare rock In such conditions, moisture retention will be impaired since there is very little soil to hold the water (made worse with chalk as it is so porous); as a result, plants are likely to suffer from summer drought. Also, pure chalk or pure rock are poor sources of plant nutrients. As an additional problem, soil over chalk is likely to be strongly alkaline, restricting the choice of plants to the most lime-tolerant.

The solution to these difficulties is simpler than you might think. Wise plant choice is the first consideration. Species which thrive in the wild on chalk downs or rocky outcrops will be natural choices and many have superb garden cultivars. Blossom trees, such as crab apples and hawthorn, do well, and among chalk-loving herbaceous plants are pinks, carnations and many campanulas.

It also makes sense to build up the topsoil as much as possible with imported material. Extra loam will help, as will generous additions of leaf mould and organic matter or manure. As for moisture retention, building up the soils humus content will enable it to hold more water, and a thick mulch of either compost, tree-bark chippings or similar material spread generously over the surface helps reduce the evaporation rate from the ground.

SHADE AND SUN

After soil type, climate and topography, comes the final key consideration: light quality. Sunlight is essential because it is absorbed by chlorophyll in the plant cells and converts moisture absorbed through the roots and carbon dioxide absorbed through the leaves into sugar and water. This vital food-making process is known as photosynthesis. Generally, the sunnier a plants position the more it reaches its full potential, but there are many notable exceptions. Thousands of plants have adapted to various kinds of shade. You only have to consider the darkness of a jungle floor and the abundance of lush vegetation growing there to realize how successful these plants are. Indeed, far from restricting choice, shade provides plenty of planting options and the chance to create a contrasting area of garden. It makes an excellent foil to bright areas with hot colours, so much so that in a large, open, sunny garden it is certainly

worth planting a small tree simply to create an area of shade to plant up accordingly.

Types of shade

Before completing a garden design, and certainly before planting, assess what kind of shade you have. The degree varies according to the amount of light received, which itself is dependent on the time of year.

Dappled shade This is thrown by the leaf canopy of trees overhead. It can be quite cool and dense in summer but non-existent in winter, and provides good woodland conditions where spring flowers bloom in full light before the tree foliage emerges.

Partial shade Such shade is created when an area is in shadow for part of the day and receives direct sunlight at other times. The further the site is from the equator, the lower the sun in winter, so that in London or Oslo, New York or Chicago, such obstacles throw more shadow than in Rome, Madrid or Los Angeles. This makes no difference in mid-winter but has a considerable influence in spring, when even as little as an hour of direct sunshine is sufficient to tempt a crocus or an aconite into bloom.

Full shade Full shade refers to an area which is always in shadow but which, nevertheless, has enough diffused daylight to support a reasonable plant collection. For example, the space between two buildings might be in constant shadow, as would the area of ground directly behind a wall running east to west (this, in turn, produces a cooler microclimate).

Dense shade This type of shade is the most likely to cause problems. There may appear to be too much gloom to grow anything but the dullest evergreen which even then languishes and looks miserable. But even dense shade is plantable.

The most challenging problem is dense, dry shade where surrounding buildings also restrict the amount of rainfall. Although there are plants that will cope with such surroundings, they seldom look as good as when growing in more suitable locations. There are, however, ways of minimizing the disadvantages. Container-grown plants can be moved here for a number of hours each day, provided at other times they get plenty of sun. Another good choice is spring bulbs which have their own food supplies and flower well in their first season even in the densest shade, but they must be replaced each year since they are unlikely to bloom again. Improving the soil to minimize moisture loss and maximize fertility will also help.

Reducing shade

There are three particularly useful ways to minimize the presence of shade. They are garden design, tree selection and tree thinning.

Garden design One of the side effects of creating shelter is that windbreaks may well impede light. This is particularly so if they enclose a garden that is long and thin and that runs east-west, and if they are approximately 5ft (1.5m) high. The solution involves a compromise between wind shelter, creating privacy and letting in daylight. One obvious answer, if the site is large enough, is to enclose part of the garden creating sheltered private shade, while leaving the remainder more open to ensure higher light levels. Alternatively, use trelliswork above a low white wall.

Tree selection Since evergreens create permanent shade, they frequently make it impossible to grow plants beneath them. Deciduous trees let in winter light, but the choice of species makes an enormous difference. Those which come into leaf late create better lighting conditions beneath their canopies. *Robinia pseudoacacia*, for example, does not begin to sprout until late spring and even then its foliage is frail and lacy, letting in a fair amount of daylight until it is fully developed in mid-summer. Large-leaved trees such as paulownia and catalpa also open late but they produce a dense canopy.

Tree thinning Many trees lend themselves to artistic pruning, which is another means of reducing the effect of dappled shade. With practice it is possible to remove whole branches cleanly instead of crudely lopping off their ends, producing a shapely, balanced tree with a smaller, more open arrangement of limbs. Please note this can be tough, even dangerous work, and you may prefer to employ a professional tree surgeon or a very experienced gardener.

Plant selection

There is a far wider choice of plants for cool, moist, woodland-type shade than for the dense dry kind, but in both cases the same planting principles apply. Since shady areas are usually sheltered from the wind, plants with large, soft leaves can be selected, with special attention to contrasting textures and colours. A light touch is necessary to avoid fussiness. A good example of plant combination features the broad, blue-green foliage of the plantain lily, *Hosta sieboldiana* (which produces violet flowers in late summer), spreading in front of the feathery fronds of the Lady fern, *Athyrium filix-femina*. Place an evergreen shrub

at the back, perhaps a camellia or a *Mahonia japonica* for its fragrant, primrose-coloured, winter flowers and glossy foliage, and complete the picture with a foreground cover of sweet violets.

Flowers that open in shade are plentiful but try to select pale colours because they show up much better than do dark reds and blues. Subtle suffusions of pink, mauve or cream, lost in full light, are more obvious in darker areas, so use plants whose flowers exhibit gentle contrasts and harmonies of hue rather than stark differences. Furthermore, since the air is often still in shady areas, scent tends to linger. This is the ideal site for a good range of fragrant plants like honeysuckle and lilies in pots which can be moved here from sunnier areas for at least part of the day. Plants for dry shade are few and far between, and in really severe cases there is not much choice. You could train a white *Clematis montana* over the offending wall, or try *Euphorbia amygdaloides robbiae* beneath it, with *Iris foetidissima*. Bulbs are the best idea, particularly beneath deciduous trees, with Solomon's seal, lily-of-the-valley and bluebells.

Left: Viburnum plicatum 'Mariesii' is sufficiently shade-tolerant to thrive at the edge of a light woodland, where its dazzling white flowers make a fine display in late spring.

Below: The best plants for hot, sunny borders are those with bright, vibrant flowers, the colours of which would be too harsh to use in an area of soft, indirect sunlight.

Sun and heat

The diversity of planting possibilities in full light is so vast that it would be impossible to do justice to the subject here. However, it would be useful to point out some of the hundreds of plants that tolerate extremes of heat and drought. The base of a sunny wall, a dry bank, and the "hot" side of a rock garden provide conditions which suit the kinds of plants that grow naturally in the maquis of the Mediterranean and the semi-desert-like conditions in Australia and North America. Such plants, with their toughened, often silvery foliage, easily cope with heat.

Many have beautiful, distinctive flowers, others have stately architectural shapes. The tall, creamy spikes of yuccas, for example, make superb living sculptures in a garden and are fully drought-tolerant.

Below: Many of the silver-grey-leaved herbs and shrubs such as lavender, thyme, rosemary and cystus thrive in dry Mediterranean-type conditions. The feathery, much divided foliage of santolina, for example, is able to resist water evaporation from its surface.

Most of the wormwoods (artemisias) have filigree foliage in silvery tones, and gems like the delicate-flowered *Convolvulus cneorum* are exquisite with their silver foliage and pinkish-white blooms.

Many bulbs and corms thrive in hot, dry conditions too, from Mediterranean anemones and dwarf irises to various green, brown and purple fritillary species. Later in the season, the alliums relish heat, as do autumn-flowering amaryllis and crinum.

Left: Tall evergreen hedges provide shade in hot areas where plants like agapanthus thrive. These do well in climates with hot, dry summers and some winter rainfall.

Below: Yew makes a dark, dense boundary, ideal for dividing up a garden. Easily clipped to provide sharp definition, it also provides a perfect backdrop for plants.

Garden designers are now very fond of pointing out that the garden is an extension of the house. The term extra room keeps cropping up. But which room? One in which to rest and relax, enjoy a barbecue, grow vegetables, play games and sports, or build up a specialist collection of plants? In a large garden the problem does not exist – the only concern is how much space to assign to each room, and how to divide the one from the other. But with a smaller area you simply have to be ruthless, limiting yourself to one or two rooms, and be particularly crafty, accepting the need for compromise. The less space there is to play with, the more ingenious the design must be.

The potager is a brilliant example of a dual-purpose room. The word means a decorative or ornamental kitchen garden, and features different-coloured vegetables (for example the reddish leaves of 'Lollo Rosso' lettuces as well as the traditional green), herbs (basil 'Ruffles Green' and 'Ruffles Purple'), and flowers. Herbaceous penstemons come in a wide range of colours from white (*Penstemon* 'Snowflake')

The Mediterranean look Gardens with a reliably dry, bright, sloping area are ideal for a wide range of scented Mediterranean shrubs like lavender, myrtle, thyme and rosemary (both the upright forms and the trailing *Rosmarinus officinalis* 'Prostratus'). Many cystus do equally well in such conditions (for example, *C. crispus*, which has grey foliage, and *C. albidus*, with leaves verging on white).

Unless you can guarantee frost-free conditions over winter the tender, heat-loving plants will have to be put into containers and brought inside. This is certainly true of *Nerium oleander*, which is never going to be as big in temperate regions as one growing in the Mediterranean or California where it makes a massive flowering hedge; even so it is definitely worth its place on a hot patio.

Some plants, like the prolific, white-flowering *Osteospermum ecklonis*, can be risked outside over winter in most areas except for the very coldest, but it is still best to take cuttings in case the temperatures dip well below freezing and kill the parent plant.

Besides the ornamental plants, also consider fruit bushes like *Citrus limon* 'Meyer'. Discovered in China at the turn of the century, it gives good-sized fruit and is hardy enough to stand outside even in a disappointing summer. In contrast, the European olive tree can be surprisingly hardy, and ought to be grown more widely in unusually warm city centres.

HOUSE AND GARDEN

Having assessed the garden's advantages and disadvantages, the next task is to consider your special needs and what you want from the garden as a space and as a reflection of your lifestyle.

to dark purple (*P*. 'Blackbird') and bloom from mid-summer until late autumn, even early winter in mild seasons. They mix well with vegetables, are usually contained in separate beds, and can be set off with topiary; for example, balls of clipped box in Versailles tubs. The Renaissance garden at Villandry in France has a particularly good formal potager and, although it is enormous, it is worth visiting to see how many ideas can be incorporated in a far smaller garden.

The second kind of compromise means beginning with one kind of garden, say predominantly lawn where children and animals can play, later converting it into another when there is no longer risk of damage to plants. Lawn can easily be replaced with paving and flower beds. The one advantage of making such changes is that at least you have time to visit scores of different gardens and work out exactly what kind of look you finally want, and the most appropriate combination of plants that will achieve these ends.

The third compromise involves children. Beware of ponds since a person can drown in even a few inches of water. Instead, use a water feature which has no

Left: Whether admiring the garden from inside or looking at the house from the garden, conservatories make the perfect link between the two, especially when packed full of plants.

Right: The design of this garden has been worked around an existing tree, which has become a central feature of a reworked site, providing an air of maturity to an otherwise new scheme.

depth: a fountain dribbling into a dish in the wall for instance, or a cascade which disappears into stones.

Planting

In small gardens the most important rule is that each and every plant must earn its keep. Only the best forms should be planted and your choice should be tempered by such questions as: Will this plant give more than one display? Does it repeat flower? What is it like in winter? Are there good seed heads, or fruits as well as spring or summer blossom? What is its autumn foliage like? Does it have good scent?

Good planting and clever design should allure, keeping the visitors curiosity alive. What goes on behind that screen? Where does this path lead? What is that flash of pink in the shrubbery? As you move around the garden you want to create changing moods and styles. Part of the key is sensitive, imaginative planting, but having learnt the basic rules do not be afraid to play with and even break them. Try introducing a few surprises. For instance, an ivy-leaved pelargonium can easily be turned into topiary. Grow a single stem up a 4ft (1.2m) high cane and then around a circular piece of bamboo attached to the top. Or create a yellow area and finish it off in high style with pots of *Lilium* 'Citronella' which twirl butterfly-like flowers to a height of 4ft (1.2m).

Linking house and garden

From indoors, the view through the windows into the garden is at least as important as the view from any vantage point outside. The garden design must therefore include vistas or scenes which look tempting from inside, from the room where you spend most time. If you are lucky enough to look out over open countryside or a fine cityscape, make sure the garden design blends with the background, for example, in a wild valley a cottage garden is most appropriate.

Looking back to the house from the garden, it should be an integral part of the design and not an alien presence. A conservatory, for instance, can be designed to open on to a terrace or patio so that in summer, when the doors are open, the garden feels as though it is extending into the house and vice versa.

Climbers and wall plants can soften the harsh outline of a building and, where pergolas lead to and echo the style and fabric of the house, the link between indoors and outdoors is sealed.

INHERITED FEATURES

In some way it is best to begin with a bare site. You can more or less do what you like with it, providing there are no overwhelming restrictions.

Far trickier is reworking an established garden. But before you demolish it, do wait one full season to see just what is there. It really is essential. Even the apparently most hideous layout is likely to have some feature worth preserving, though it may not be immediately obvious. Note down the existing spring bulbs, shrubs for winter colour, colourful autumn seedheads, boggy winter areas, particularly dry hot summer beds and then you can decide which features to keep.

Plants

In the case of an overgrown garden, dig out known weeds and give established plants a chance to show what they can do. In cases of serious neglect this may be difficult because of the urgent need for renovation, but even so it pays to be circumspect.

Overgrown shrubs and trees can be pruned and tidied up without damage indeed many shrubs respond well to being cut hard back. Furthermore, do not be afraid to impose shape on the apparently shapeless. The Japanese are particularly good at it. For example, *Ceanothus thyrsiflorus* can be converted from shrubbiness to a shapely, weeping tree. Again, *Prunus laurocerasus* 'Magnifolia' can be turned from a floppy specimen into something more statuesque and

GARDEN DESIGNS: SITE
ONE (right and far right)
A south-facing garden,
20 × 50ft (6 × 15m), with a
slight slope from north to
south. Neutral soil.

upright. When it comes to transplanting, mature woody plants can be difficult, but perennials are easy to lift, divide and replant into temporary nursery beds, perhaps while new borders are being laid out. In such cases, it pays to plan a new design carefully, to avoid heaving up plants again.

Large natural features

Objects such as large trees or natural water courses, which make prominent features, could push you on to the horns of a dilemma: how will they look when incorporated into a new design? It is impossible to suggest general solutions, but the basis for your decision should be tempered by the following considerations: is the tree or natural feature particularly fine, rare or special in any other way? Could you reshape your design to work around the feature? Since maturity is lacking in a new garden, and since the established look is going to be the aim, is it possible to keep the feature for the medium term until the garden has mellowed and matured, and then think about replacing it with a specimen tree or sculpture?

Structural and ornamental features

Hard landscaping and architectural and ornamental features present less of a problem than natural features because in most cases they can be dismantled and relocated. The advantage of re-using such existing materials stone walls and troughs, paving slabs, millstones and so on is that they will be weathered and worn, as compared to the rather sterile appearance of new materials. If you want to dispose of existing features, it is worth looking to auction houses to sell ornaments and the small advertisements in local newspapers and magazines for building materials. Many garden details have a surprising value.

TIME AND MONEY

The joy of gardening is that it suits every pocket. Landscaping a small area with choice materials and lavish, mature plants is expensive; by contrast, using inexpensive materials, propagating as many plants as possible and being prepared to wait is the best way to develop a fine garden on a shoestring.

Interim measures have their uses: beds can be filled with annuals until you can afford more expensive shrubs; an arrangement of pots can provide the focal point until a statue or sculpture has been added. For example, an architectural *Cordyline indivisa* can be set in a tall or raised pot with pots of scented flowering

INFORMAL GARDEN

This design recaptures the spirit of an old cottage garden, using both traditional and modern plant species, combined with natural materials. The landscaping is of blue-grey stone, slate and gravel; most of the pathways are designed to allow plants to spill over at either side. The east-facing wall includes (top to bottom) *Pittosporum* 'Garnetti', *Polygonatum × hybridum*, *Rheum alexandrae*, *Hosta sieboldiana*, *Lupinus* 'Inverewe Red', *Amelanchier lamarckii*, *Papaver bracteatum* 'Goliath' and *Thalictrum delavayi*. An apple tree provides a focal point; underplanting includes *Milium effusum*. *Verbascum olympicum* and *Digitalis purpurea* 'Alba' give height to the bed beyond the terrace, which is lined with tubs of fragrant *Lilium regale*. A cold frame, compost container and shed are set apart.

FORMAL GARDEN

A linear, symmetrical form has been given to the space by means of clearly defined surfaces and structures and controlled planting. The terrace is framed by ivy, ferns and containers planted with *Trachycarpus fortunei*; this has an architectural quality. The facing benches lead the eye into the garden. The small parterre is planted with *Buxus sempervirens*, which will frame seasonal planting in restricted colours. Bay trees (*Laurus nobilis*) sit at each corner. The central, raised summer house gives a focus to the vista; espalier pears or pleached quince are trained at either side. A well-clipped *Taxus baccata* hedge encloses a seat and hides the compost area and cloches at the end of the garden. *Actinidia kolomikta* plants shroud the greenhouse and shed. The surfaces are yellow-ochre gravel and pink granite.

heliotropium, such as the fine 'Chatsworth', 'Princess Marina' or 'White Lady', and the yellow-orange flowers of echeveria around the base.

From the gardening point of view phasing the work has many advantages, but the question is which major structures should you complete first? Clearly the answer depends on your own priorities but it is logical to begin with the basic layout. Lawns, pathways, main borders and the seating area provide the garden skeleton and take priority. Later, when your pocket has recovered, you can add a little more flesh to the bones by adding special features like a pond, conservatory, gazebo and so on. Usually, the biggest cost item is the hard landscaping: structures such as walls, terraces, buildings and paving. There may be earth-moving exercises too, such as digging ponds or creating different levels. These, especially if done by contractors, will be costly but are one-off expenses.

Inexpensive plants

Mature trees are the costliest plants to buy, and the bigger they are, the dearer. In effect you are buying the time taken to grow specimens. If you are prepared to nurture them, most small, immature plants grow very quickly and are much cheaper. The important point to remember is that they will grow just as large as their bigger, more expensive counterparts, and need spacing out according to their potential and not their current size.

The cheapest plants of all are those that you propagate yourself. Shrubs grow surprisingly fast from cuttings and many are easy to root. Space is too limited to cover the subject here but there are dozens of specialist books on propagation, so do have a go. The skill needed to strike cuttings is so basic that anyone can learn it in minutes. Essentially, all that is required is a piece of healthy young stem, a pot of compost and a warm, moist atmosphere that prevents the shoot wilting. Within a few weeks you should have a new plant.

A clear plastic bag and a windowsill will suffice for small numbers of cuttings, but results are quicker and better with an electrically-heated propagator. The most basic types are widely available in a range of sizes and are easily affordable. The crudest consist of a large open tray with low sides, a plastic cover and a heating pad. If you have a cold frame or a cold greenhouse you can wait for decent summer temperatures around 60°F (15.5°C) and raise cuttings there. Place them in a sheltered, shady position and remember to close the greenhouse to keep in the heat. A cold frame is not essential when it comes to acclimatizing the

GARDEN DESIGNS: SITE
TWO (right and far right)
A west-facing walled garden,
20 x 20ft (6 x 6m). Acid soil.

CONTAINER GARDEN

Shrub roses, small rhododendrons and foliage plants set off the containers in this grotto-like space. The late spring display shows blue hyacinths and white and pink tulips on a gravel sweep. (In summer impatiens, lilies and fuchsias can be used; in autumn, dahlias.) Pots of *Phygelius aequalis* 'Yellow Trumpet' stand either side of the large *Acer japonicum* 'Aureum'; herbs and ferns are placed beside the house. The central feature has four specimens of the evergreen *Ligustrum japonicum*, with hydrangeas in the middle (bergenias in winter) and gap-filling *Alchemilla mollis*.

young plants to outside conditions but it helps. Alternatively, stand the pots outside for an increasing amount of time during the warmest part of the day, and eventually you should be able to leave them out over a mild night before planting them out completely, but do not rush the process.

Nor should you be afraid to ask neighbours for cuttings of various plants or for seed. You should have a good success rate with both, as with layering (bending a branch down to the soil level, pegging it in place, waiting for it to develop its own root system, and then separating this new, young plant from its parent), dividing one plant into several smaller ones (each with its own top growth and roots), and stooling (building up soil around the base of a japonica or lilac, for example, which encourages rooting higher up the stem so that ready-rooted pieces can easily be removed and replanted).

MAINTENANCE

The labour-free garden does not exist, but there are ways in which such chores as weeding and tidying can be kept to a minimum.

Clearly, what you get out of a garden is in proportion to what you put in, and it will never be possible to expect a plantsman's paradise to thrive on neglect. Those who want beauty without effort are being unrealistic, but there is no need to become a slave. Any means of reducing the more troublesome tasks to a minimum is worth pursuing.

Design

Much labour can be saved by thoughtful design. All parts of a border, for example, should be accessible without having to walk on and damage the soil surface. This is achieved by laying stepping stones or pathways along the back as well as in the more visible areas. Paving is easier to maintain than lawn and, in a small garden, flagstones can look better than grass.

Gravel, as a mulching device, is gaining popularity, easing maintenance and providing plants with a friendly environment. Plants growing in gravel or shingle seed freely; to prevent this, lay the mulch over a woven polypropylene sheet; water will still pass through. To plant shrubs or specimens, a crisscross slit is made in the sheet, the plant inserted and the gravel carefully replaced.

The vertical surfaces in a well-planned garden will be covered with a wealth of climbing and wall plants. To encourage them to grow up and sideways and not flop over the plants in front of them, tie in all growths to horizontal wires. These should be attached to vine eyes or large nails inserted into the masonry at regular intervals. With this permanent anchorage, it is easy to display wall plants to their best advantage.

Planting

Choice of plants and their arrangement exert an enormous influence on the amount of time needed for maintenance. The aim in a carefree garden is to make the plants themselves do as much work as possible.

MODERN GARDEN

The theme here is cool greens and whites, with scented flowers for evening entertaining. Marbled tiles swirl around a fibreglass table and seat, protected by a parasol (cut away in this view). The planting uses tender species, including *Lonicera splendida*, *Hedera helix* 'Telecurl' and *Wisteria floribunda* 'Alba' around the walls. The central beds have a pleasing symmetry: *Ficus benjamina* with its variegated form grow hydroponically in the raised triangle; *Camellia japonica* 'Commander Mulroy', *Phanerophlebia falcata* and nicotiana are either side of a raised mirror pool.

Thus, shrubs which need little pruning are preferable to those like hybrid tea roses which require more attention. Disease- and pest-resistant plants will always be desirable and, unless a species is especially glorious, vigour takes preference over delicacy.

Among herbaceous varieties, those which self-seed freely without becoming invasive are ideal in the low-maintenance garden. Ground-cover plants are perfect for filling the spaces between shrubs and give excellent weed control, provided the ground in which they are planted is completely free of perennial weeds. There are so many to choose from that dull planting is inexcusable. It is perfectly possible to arrange a weed-proof ground cover which changes in colour, texture and mood, month by month.

STARTING THE DESIGN

Once you know all about your site, exactly what you want from your garden, what inherited features are worth preserving and how much time you want to spend on maintenance, you can begin the design. To do this you will need squared or graph paper and a pencil, but to generate any useful ideas, first stand in the garden or on the patch that is to become your garden and think. Turn the area into a dream space in your mind's eye. Think not of specific plants but in terms of shapes and colours. As ideas begin to form, you can then explore practicalities and solve problems. Finally, you should measure the plot and trim your dream to fit the area, and your pocket.

Preparing the plan

The practical business of designing – preparing drawings to scale, organizing plant lists, and so on – appears to be far more daunting than it really needs to be. Accuracy is important but it is not that difficult to achieve; if you are methodical and careful, the site can be measured and a true plan drawn. You should include all important details: architectural features, the herb garden, beds and borders, pond, large trees, topiary, key shrubs, and the like. If you find it difficult to visualize designs from lines on a piece of paper, there is really no reason why you should not use the garden itself as your drawing board. The site, if not already clean, will have to be cleared of any rubbish or unwanted objects before you begin. Then, using sticks and lengths of string (preferably strong and very visible baler twine) as markers, it is possible to indicate where everything should go. Keep making adjustments to these markers until you have the layout you want. A length of hosepipe is very useful for marking out curving border fronts. I certainly feel much more comfortable working on the design in the garden itself, juggling my sticks, string and hosepipe until I feel I have laid out all the features and details in the best order and proportions.

Complicated details like a parterre may require a more striking outline. This can be achieved with whitewash brushed over the grass or surface of the proposed location. Eccentric though this may sound, any step between planning and planting is invaluable and

WOODLAND GARDEN

Tranquil woodland gardens come into their own in spring, when
bulbs and woodland herbaceous plants provide a riot of colour,
as here. The two pin oaks, *Quercus palustris*, are about fifteen
years old but will cast only dappled shade even when mature
(they are cut away to reveal the underplanting). The right-hand
tree stands in front of a hedge of *Prunus spinosa*; a drift of yellow
Primula vulgaris sweeps up into the garden, past a dark holly.
Corsican pines (*Pinus nigra*), three *Betula utilis jacquemontii*
and an *Acer saccharum* 'Temples Upright' are surrounded
by cyclamen, honesty and bluebells. A stile leads into a
wood beyond. On the other side of the path a *Crataegus
oxycantha* 'Plena' is grouped with three *Hamamelis ×
intermedia* 'Jelena'. Beneath the second oak tree is an
Epimedium × perralchicum, surrounded by trillium,
bluebells, foxgloves and ferns. Primulas and hazels grow
beside the gate. Around the log bench are snowdrops,
chamomile and *Rosa rugosa* 'Fru Dagmar Hastrup'. The
natural-looking pond is planted with yellow *Primula
florindae*, giant cowslips and *Myosotis scorpioides*.

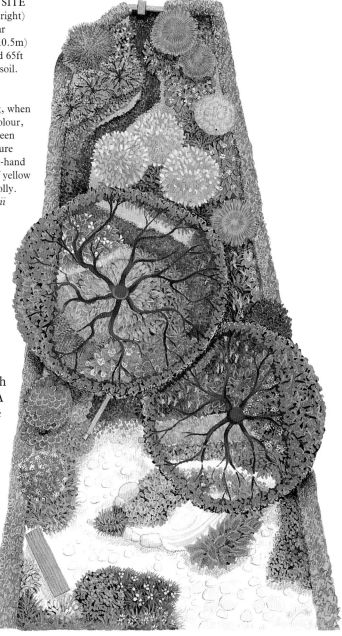

saves subsequent heartache. It is also worth
visualizing height where this is a vital factor. A
stepladder erected to the height of a mature
hedge will give you a good idea of the ultimate
effect. If this looks too tall, obscuring a fine
view and casting too much shade, select a different hedging plant. Again, if you intend to
include a lengthy pergola, you could draw on
a clever technique of an earlier era. In the
1920s, wealthy house owners placed card-
board cut-out pillars in various positions
until they looked exactly right. Another
eccentricity, but useful and potentially
great fun if enough people are involved.
Improvise in such a manner wherever possible: put a chair in a proposed seating area
and try it out. Is this the best place, or will it
be ruined by an unpleasant view?

When you have a clearer idea of the arrangement of
your site it will be easier to transfer the details onto
paper; this will be essential for reference once the
heavy work has begun. Before you draw up the plan,
leave the markers in place for a week or so to ensure
that the idea really is going to be practical. Then,
when you are finally happy with the main elements of
the design, draw up the plan.

The proposed planting

With the outline in hand, start filling in planting
details on the plan shapes, colours, texture and scent,
leaving the choice of most plants until last. Scent is
most easily dealt with. Tobacco plants, pots of lilies,
Choisya ternata and the like, need to be in sheltered
positions where the fragrance will hang in still air.
Ideally such plants should surround the seating and
eating areas where they are really going to be appreciated. A bench or patio can be backed by a semi-
circular enclosing trellis threaded with scented
climbers. The plants should be chosen so they flower
in succession right through the summer and you get a
prolonged spell of delightful perfumes, not one over-
powering blast for two weeks in August.

The next stage is to ensure that the planting line-up
is going to provide colour and interesting shapes right
through the year. Use four different-coloured pens
(signifying winter, spring, summer and autumn) to
mark blocks of plants on the plan and, if possible,
grow a star plant for every season in each area. (When
planting, leave space around the young specimens to

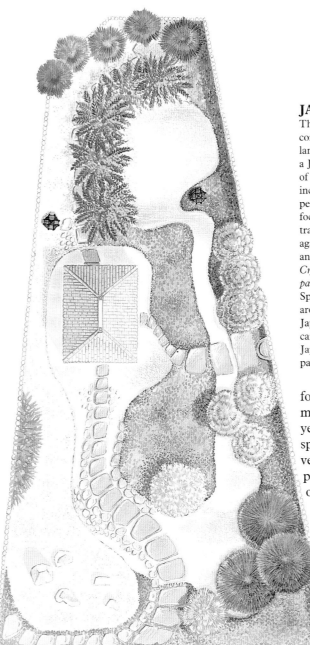

JAPANESE GARDEN

The distinctive flavour of a Japanese garden is achieved by combining a traditional layout with special features, such as lanterns and a washing basin (included here) and sculpture with a Japanese theme: dragons, temples and shrines, all of which are of symbolic value. This strictly contrived, restful landscape includes the central elements of water and rocks, making a perfect setting for the small tea house which provides a charming focal point. Opposites run through the design, with moving and tranquil water, jagged rocks versus smooth boulders, and gravel against moss. The planting is essentially Japanese in the selection and groupings. Around the water, from the house front, a *Cryptomeria japonica* 'Vilmoriniana' leads to groups of *Pinus parviflora*, *Acer palmatum* 'Ozakazuki' and *A. p.* 'Senkaki'. Spring-flowering white cherries (*Prunus* 'Tai-Haku') curve around the top of the pool, with a strong accent supplied by the Japanese black pines (*Pinus thunbergii*). Bamboo is used in a tied cane fence and as a planted hedge and curving clump. However, Japanese gardens can take a long time to mature; they demand patience and careful training.

focal points, having the additional benefit of a dramatic flowering spike something like once every 20 years! Much smaller but also effective are the white spotted leaves of *Pulmonaria longifolia* and the velvety, light grey foliage of *Stachys byzantina*, appropriately called lambs tongue or rabbits ears. Hunt out other eye-catching examples.

Construction

With your well-considered plan complete, work can begin. Borders can be dug out, areas for lawns dug, raked and rolled and foundations for paving installed. All the time this is going on, keep reviewing the scene and be prepared to make any changes that might occur to you. This is much easier to do at the outset than later when more permanent construction is under way. With regard to heavy equipment, you should always be sure to hire well-maintained, modern and safe machinery. Make sure you fully understand how to use it, taking all necessary precautions, and leave no harmful devices to hand for inquisitive children to discover.

Needless to say, there is always the option of using a professional garden designer and a contractor. If you have ambitious plans, limited time or an aversion to hard physical work, such experts should be seriously considered. Their involvement could raise the cost of a project quite dramatically, but equally costly mistakes could be avoided. You will not have the complete satisfaction of knowing that all you survey is your work, but you might have come that much nearer to achieving your dream garden. It is a matter of weighing up the advantages and disadvantages to

accommodate their ultimate spread. Annuals and bedding plants can fill the gaps temporarily.) Many gardeners are drawn to the idea of an all-white garden at some point, but it is important to remember that they generate a lot of extra work as faded blooms present a glaring eyesore.

Foliage

One key point rarely mentioned is that most plants only flower for a relatively short period, which means foliage and shape ought to be rated just as highly as flowering interest. Palm trees are impressive on both counts. They *do* grow in mild areas, with the advantage that their fronds will not turn the frazzled brown seen in hotter climates. Alternatively, agaves are much hardier than generally realized and make good

both approaches. A good garden designer will be sensitive to your preferences and tastes as well as to the context: the style of your house and the surrounding view, quite apart from the size, shape and contours of the space involved.

Perhaps the key point about a garden is that it is never complete. As with a sitting room, owners occasionally get bored with a particular look and rearrange things. Then, a plant that succeeded in its previous place may, for no known reason, fail in the new, apparently more appropriate site. Another plant must

be sought, and the colour scheme suddenly leaps from pink to yellow and different, complementary features become desirable. It is a matter of being aware of the alternatives and gauging whether they can be made to work. The six garden designs included on these pages give you some impression of the range of options available. The idea is not to copy them slavishly – some of the design elements are solutions to very specific problems – but to apply similar principles of design to your garden to suit the prevailing conditions and serve your own needs and tastes.

Left: What makes this garden so satisfying is the definite lines of its underlying structure. All hard landscaping and trellising must be planned and constructed before any planting is undertaken.

Right: Flowers need not feature in a border. Foliage is the central component of this garden: cool and restrained, the use of ferns and grasses capitalizes on the great variety of leaf shapes.

Below: With such variety of plant material, it takes a very skilled gardener to make a satisfying overall effect like this. Most plans are far simpler initially, although they may evolve with time.

THE LOOK
OF THE
GARDEN

SHAPES

The use of different shapes is perhaps the single most important element in designing a garden. It is the chief tool with which a gardener defines the spaces and structures of a garden – his working vocabulary. In a really good garden, consideration will have been given to the shape and purpose of every component, from broad issues such as the outline of a path or lawn to the details such as the contrasting shapes of miniature shrubs in a particular stone trough. It is the sum of all these parts, large and small, which gives a garden its character.

The garden's perimeter is the first shape to consider in relation to the site as a whole. The internal structure can complement the shape through a geometrical composition, using straight lines and circles, with the emphasis on hard landscaping (the walls, paths, steps and so on). Alternatively, natural flowing forms with no straight lines may be preferred. Again, a blend of the two approaches might be more suitable. In making this decision, the practical requirements of the garden must be considered: the need to get from one place to another, to create enclosures and the like. All the components of a garden – from lawns, borders, island beds and parterres to paths, topiary, pergolas and water features – can be treated in a geometric or an organic way. There is no right or wrong, only a variety of options with which the imagination can experiment.

Within the layout, the shape of the plants themselves comes into play. All plants fall into one of a number of basic shape categories, the plants in each category fulfilling a similar role in the overall scheme. There is the tall upright shape of fastigiate trees and conifers which leads the eye upwards and commands

Left and right: The first shapes to consider in a garden are those of the ground plan. Here, two perfectly geometric schemes are achieved, one by the formal planting of hedges and lawns, the other largely by the use of hard landscaping. Both gardens show remarkable attention to the detail of shapes. The planting is noteworthy. An orderly yet imaginative series of beds compares with symmetrical but strong forms that soften the modern design.

Below: A woodland garden begins life under mature trees, on organic rather than geometric lines. Unless the shapes of an organic plan are broad and simple, the effect is fussy and appears just as contrived as a formal garden, even though the scheme is non-symmetrical.

Top far left, top left and right: Strong shapes, such as tall upright conifers, make an even greater impact when repeated, and usually strong horizontals and more earthbound shapes are needed to balance the effect. Horizontal lines of great substance are most often gained from hard landscaping, such as walls and paths, reinforced by plants with a naturally tiered, architectural habit, or those that have been trained to form striking, flattened shapes. Notice the clever use of an espalier-trained weeping blue cedar (*top left*). The combination of horizontal and vertical lines will weave a design together, forming unifying connections. This is demonstrated by the strategically placed ornaments – the obelisk and pots – that point up from the flat lines of the retaining walls (*right*).

Bottom left: Shapes repeated often enough provide a large-scale texture, as do these domes of lavender. When shapes are repeated in a straight line, like the mounds beneath the pergola, they are almost more effective than a clean straight line in leading the eye forward. In summer, these bushes would provide a glorious, aromatic display of flowers, giving a very different face to the garden. The cypress arch and the trimmed laurels (either side of the steps) present different but connected forms. The climbing roses have an altogether freer disposition and open effect.

attention, especially when used repeatedly in a group or row. The effect is the same whatever the scale: notice how the *Kochia scoparia tricophylla*, burning bush, dominates in this way when used in a bedding scheme. Low rounded shapes or domes are equally arresting, but in a more earthbound way. They sit heavily upon the ground and fix the eye. Think of clipped spheres of box or chunky potentilla bushes. Fans or fountain shapes offer a softer touch, lifting the eye but in a gentler lighter way than a conifer. Grasses, bamboos and irises all shoot up in a fan, and many then droop over at the top, like a subsiding firework. A more extreme version of this effect is the weeping shape, less visually static than the sphere and less busy than the fountain. Finally, there are the horizontal shapes, found in plants like the architec-

tural *Viburnum plicatum* 'Mariesii', *Cornus controversa* and some of the low junipers, for example *Juniperus horizontalis* and *J. × media* 'Pfitzeriana'. They keep the eye peacefully arrested, moving neither up nor down, forwards nor backwards. Obviously there are endless variations within and between these categories, but when planning a layout they are very useful tool.

It is the arrangement of these typical shapes that gives movement, balance and punctuation to a garden design. For example, movement can come from the repeated use of upright shapes which takes the eye away into the distance. The effect will work either in a formal symmetrical context, as in an avenue, or in a more informal zigzag fashion. Balance will help the garden to look restful to the eye. For instance, a dramatic upright shape can be countered by an adjoining

Below: The main contrasting elements here are the fans of iris leaves, the closed shape of a clipped euonymus and the airy form of the variegated *Acer negundo* trees.

Top right: Shape is relevant in every aspect of the garden. It is expressed in the ground plan – lawns, beds, borders, paths, hedges, walls and containers. Also important are the outlines of single plants and groups of plants, and even the shape of flowers. Shape, however, must work hand in glove with texture and colour: none exists in isolation.

Bottom right: Much can be made of the interaction of colour and shape. A sombre walk of tall cypresses is brightened and balanced by a horizontal streak of pebbles.

low mound, and the two held together by some horizontal shapes. Strong shapes can be used to focus and punctuate the different areas within a garden, perhaps by closing an avenue with a tight specimen tree or by flanking a gateway with two strong mounds or sentinels of foliage.

Apart from these structural uses of shape, a garden is kept alive through its detail, by the constant interplay between neighbouring plants. Shape is just as important here as texture or colour. It is the continuous interplay between shape, colour and texture which makes a mixed or herbaceous border so fascinating, and so difficult to achieve over a long period, presenting a challenge to the gardener.

It is often helpful in the planning stages of a garden, or even a border, to make simple sketches that block in the most important shapes and lines (as well as the main colour effects). This will enable you to envisage the composition in advance and allows the main refinements to be made before planting begins. It is also useful for considering the mature aspect of the garden, which should include appropriate spacing of trees and large shrubs. This is an excellent tool for clarifying your ideas; on paper, the imagination can run riot, but once planting begins, changes become much more difficult. A plan can bring you that much closer to your ideal, well balanced garden. (See page 27 for further advice on starting the design.)

CONTOURS

Not everyone is blessed with an easy, level site for a garden, and those who are often long for a more varied terrain. Whatever your preference, there is no doubt that level ground makes gardening easier and that changes of level create a set of problems, both in planting and with access. But however steep the site, so long as you work within its limitations, it is perfectly possible to have an interesting and fulfilling garden. Virtue must be made of necessity.

Steeply sloping gardens lend themselves to different treatments depending upon their aspect. South-facing slopes receive the maximum heat from the sun and are especially suitable for Mediterranean plants or make good scree gardens. Drainage will be fast, which is an advantage to many slightly tender plants. These slopes also offer the possibility of creating streams or waterfalls, which can be made to be as formal or informal as required. Terraces can be constructed across the slope, as in the great villa gardens of Italy, to maximize the potential for planting, using either retaining walls or turf banks.

Cold north-facing slopes make good woodland gardens, but will equally make an ideal site for a terraced alpine garden because they are naturally well drained, fully exposed to light, but without the drying heat found on a south-facing slope.

The approach used on a sloping site also depends on its relationship to the house. A garden that slopes up from the house will be far more dominant than one that slopes away: it will fill the whole view and offer the opportunity for a real *tour de force*, whether formal or informal. It could be perfectly symmetrical with pairs of circular steps or an idealized Japanese mountain waterfall. Sites which slope away from the house are less imposing in themselves and throw the eye outwards into the view beyond. It might be Mount Fuji, a power station or just your neighbour's garden. Whether this view should be incorporated

into the garden's design or excluded to produce an enclosed oasis will depend on its merits or demerits. If the view is good, and it can be relied upon to remain so, then make the most of it. If the focus needs to be kept within the garden then try using a formal arrangement of large pots or upright conifers. These may not mask a poor view but they will give details of some substance to attract the eye.

Irregular changes of level within a garden can make it more interesting and offer the chance to create surprise views and features. The move from one level to another does not necessarily have to be negotiated in one go; a flight of steps can be split up and intermediate levels inserted in between. Steps are one of the most significant built features of a garden and deserve to have plenty of attention given to their detail. If the garden contains large mounds or hollows, consider enlarging them to create a major feature, such as a pond or a mount or rockery.

During the planning stage always keep in mind the maintenance implications of the finished garden. Steps are attractive, but they can stop easy access with a wheelbarrow or lawn mower. Terraces are fine, but will there be suitable access to take away prunings? Should the compost heap be positioned at the bottom or the top of the slope? Where access is limited, it is often better to opt for a style of planting that requires little pruning, such as an alpine or heather garden.

Finally, soil erosion can be a problem on banks and can be solved in a variety of ways. Turf banks will hold the soil once they are established, but ruts can soon develop where people constantly walk. Ground cover plants such as *Hypericum calycinum*, which have underground stems to bind the surface soil in a tight mat, can be used to stabilize a bank, but they may take some years to become effective. In extreme cases, terracing and channelled drainage may be essential.

Top right: Changes of level break up a garden. Here a sense of open space is retained by avoiding the use of steps and letting a grass bank link the lower and upper lawns to form one space. The grass flows around the contours.

Centre right: Terraces always present problems of access. Here a grass ramp allows a mower to be driven onto the terrace, but steps also make it visually more satisfying and close the vista.

Bottom right: A long flight of shallow steps is awkward to walk on and is generally not the best solution on a gradual slope. A path with a gentle gradient is usually more satisfactory, although you will need to make provision for water running off fast and hard when it rains. This detail is a fine illustration of a well conceived design. The mixed border has been planned to show every plant to its best advantage. It is backed by an attractive plant-clad wall.

Top left: Steps provide a good opportunity for interesting planting. There is no reason at all why you should not plant into the steps themselves, so long as they remain safe.

Top right: On terraced sites, sprawling evergreen perennials soften the edges of retaining walls, even in winter.

Above: Terrace walls and steps lend themselves easily to a very formal treatment, especially in front of an imposing symmetrical house. A formal planting with evergreens offers greater winter interest than an informal scheme. This clever planting affords very varied textures and shapes.

Opposite, top: Even in a small, flat garden changes of level can be introduced by building raised areas like this circular platform. The seat gives it an added *raison d'être*. Repeated motifs can be used in subtle ways in garden designs. The gentle bend of the steps and wall and the circles of the urns echo the curving theme.

Opposite, bottom: This grass terrace has been introduced as a means of separating the garden from grazed fields without the need for a solid, stock-proof fence. The wall has been built at an angle to help it resist the weight of soil pushing from behind. It presents a pleasing sweep, perfect for strolling along.

MANIPULATING SCALE

It is a rare gardener indeed who wishes to make a garden look smaller than it is, unless he or she is motivated by an underlying passion for bonsai landscapes. Most wish to increase the apparent size; others to make a broad site with little depth appear longer than it is, or to make a long and narrow garden seem less tunnel-like; or the aim may simply be to make a small garden seem less confined. A way to do all these things is through the manipulation of scale.

Making a small garden appear less cramped is often best achieved by avoiding a single unified design; rather, the space can be broken down into even smaller portions, where the attention is focused onto the detail of planting and hard landscaping. These spaces or garden rooms can each be given different characters which are presented as a series of little surprises. There is no golden rule which says a garden must have an open lawn in the middle; if space is really tight it is usually better to go for a fuller, heavier planting. One possibility is to turn the garden into a miniature ornamental jungle, where paths wind in among the plants in such a way as never to reveal the full extent of the site.

Long thin gardens can also be treated this way, so that it is never possible to see down the full length of the long axis. If this is unavoidable, then try to arrest the eye with some major feature in the foreground or middle distance, such as a circular lawn or a specimen tree, or place horizontal features such as low walls, wide steps, paving or hedges across the axis. Tiered plants like *Viburnum plicatum* 'Mariesii' have the same effect. In a less symmetrical garden, features can be placed down the sides, causing the eye to swerve and pause – perhaps a painted seat in a formal arbour or the striking trunks of a multi-stemmed tree. In all of this it is a good idea to begin by making a sketch plan of the garden and drawing in the sight lines to see where the visual emphasis lies.

There are many ways of increasing the sense of depth in a garden. Vistas can be emphasized and

Far left: Clever transitions, from one part to another, increase the feeling of variety and size within a garden. One area can be used like the hall of a house, giving access to different "rooms" that may or may not pick up motifs and materials from the useful linking areas.

Left: Even in informal gardens, vistas can be emphasized by careful planting. A solid screen of shrubs would be much less effective than the golden foliage and the elegant, upright blue cypress that form the focus of this vista.

Right: The lines of tile detail on this rendered wall lead the eye on and succeed in increasing the false perspective through the two arches, making the second seem further away. The glimpses of plants and steps beyond enhance this impression.

Below: The stripes produced by a lawn mower can be used to draw the eye according to the direction of the cut. Here they emphasize the vista, counteracting the cross-banding of the steps and leading the eye to the statue.

Left: Still water and the mirrored sky give a feeling of light and air, while reflections emphasize the vertical lines of upright forms. A large space that is given a carefully designed treatment needs to be handled with care to avoid great "lost" expanses jarring with highly finished parts of the garden. Transitional areas are essential in the design if the scheme is not naturally compartmentalized.

Top right: Long narrow gardens can be made more interesting by deliberately closing the central vista with a bold feature, such as this pergola, set at right angles to the main thrust of the site. This device effectively creates two separate gardens, each of which can be given a different character.

Top far right: In small gardens it is often better to dispense with views altogether and to go for a closely-planted jungle-like effect. In a garden of this scale paving makes a much better surface than lawn.

Bottom right: Foreground detail can be used to arrest the eye. Here the view to an unremarkable field is lightly screened by wonderful clipped trees and hedges so that the focus is brought forward to the circular lawn of chessmen. The large formal bands of gravel provide a border to the elaborate central design, setting apart the imaginative array of shapes more dramatically than would be achieved with grass.

"lengthened" by stressing the distant perspective. Eye-catching features can be used to draw the eye away into the distance, and there is no need to rely solely on the contents of your garden to do this. Make use of the landscape outside: let a distant hilltop or church spire become the focus of a garden vista. On the other hand, a door in a garden wall 20ft (6m) away will work in the same way for a smaller garden. It is a matter of degree and using opportunities.

Creating a false perspective is another useful technique. By placing large plants in the foreground and smaller ones of the same shape in the distance, at a glance they all appear to be the same size but receding into the distance. It is possible to do the same with foliage, by planting thin airy foliage close by and denser foliage further away.

Lawn-mower stripes in a lawn can be used to give direction to a view or to pull the eye in a particular direction, lengthening or shortening the perspective. Arches and pergolas will enhance perspective, while fences and trelliswork have a strong linear impact. Trellis can also create *trompe l'oeil* effects, giving the impression of three dimensions where only two exist. Even mirrors have been used in garden doorways to double the length of a vista. *Trompe l'oeil* can be used to highly sophisticated ends, with false scenes and features painted onto flat surfaces. Such tricks can be very restrictive to a whole design so they should be used with care. Simpler devices might be preferable; the reflective surface of a pool of still water offers tranquillity and a vertical dimension (its own depth and the reflection of the sky above).

SEASONAL PLANNING

A garden can never be as colourful in winter as in summer, but there is no reason why it should not be just as interesting but in different ways. This is simply a matter of planning so that there is always something attractive to be seen. Each season needs thinking about in terms of the colour of flowers, foliage and fruit, form, texture, perfume and the uses to which the garden will be put. Even if a grand slam of summer colour is desired, it is still possible to underplant and interplant for other times of the year.

There is almost no season in which bulbs do not flower and most of them are easy and trouble-free to grow. Use dry shade under trees for winter aconites and spring and autumn cyclamen. Plant the early dwarf daffodils and the very late, scented pheasant-eye types as well as the mid-season hybrids. Tulips in all their variety have a long season from March to May. There are spring- and autumn-flowering crocuses, as well as the colchicums (meadow saffron) which flower in September. Lilies and galtonias will fill the middle of the summer. Remember that bulbs do not need to occupy a space solely for themselves; they can be tucked in among other plants, almost as a bonus. Bulbs naturalized in grass are a delight.

Perfume can be present in the garden throughout most of the year. There are headily scented, late winter and early spring shrubs such as *Azara*, *Sarcococca*, *Chimonanthus*, *Viburnum* and *Hamamelis*. Even heather is very sweet on the air in March. Try to make room near to a door for a shrub with good perfume in winter, and have those with summer perfume by windows or sitting-out areas, especially if they produce

Left: Autumn colour should be planned for at all levels of the garden, from the tree canopy down through shrubs (such as the Japanese maple shown here), to herbaceous plants with berries or colourful foliage. It is not just trees and shrubs that colour in autumn. The foliage of herbaceous plants, including bergenias, gillenias and *Euphorbia cyparissias*, can colour just as beautifully as the leaves of the larger plants. The euphorbia, for one, also has delightful spring interest, bearing lime green flowers.

Top: Summer showpiece borders, awash with colour as here, steal all the limelight for a few months, but gardens need to compensate elsewhere to give interest throughout the year. The focus of interest can move round the garden as the year progresses.

Bottom right: In the depths of winter, late berries and flowers, coloured bark, evergreens and even snow itself lend colour to a garden. It would be hard to better these "flowers" of ice. The skeletal forms of plants are central to the winter garden.

Right: Heathers and conifers can be very bright in winter, seen in the selection here. Their evergreen colours are best woven subtly into the entire fabric of the garden.

their strongest scent in the evening. There are also plants with scented foliage to consider, such as *Artemisia abrotanum* (ladslove) and *Helichrysum italicum* (the curry plant).

In many places herbaceous perennials can be found in flower for almost 11 months out of the 12, and by planting a good cross section it is possible to get a long season. Hellebores are invaluable in late winter and are soon followed by pulmonarias. Both of these have an unseasonal lushness. Spring and summer are well supplied with colourful perennials, but there are plenty more which flower in the autumn such as *Rudbeckia*, *Persicaria*, *Schizostylis*, michaelmas daisies and dahlias.

In the winter the focus shifts to evergreen foliage, and there is a great variety of textures and colours to choose from including the glossy spiny leaves of holly, the soft gold of some variegated yews, or the blue of

spruce needles. The interest supplied by coloured bark is also invaluable. Stooled dogwoods offer scarlet, purple and yellow bark; while that of willows is orange, bloomy grey or glossy brown. Some species of birch have brilliant white or coppery-pink bark and there are cherries with glorious, dramatic bark of purest polished mahogany.

Autumn colour can be found in trees like maples and rowans, but there are vines of equal brilliance and even herbaceous plants such as euphorbia and gillenia. Fruits and berries need not just be an autumn feature. Many roses carry their hips and *Mahonia aquifolium* bears its blue berries in late summer. Later come the reds, yellows and oranges of holly, rowans, cotoneasters and pyracantha. Usually the paler the berry, the later the birds will descend to eat them.

In winter a garden falls back on its structure to make itself interesting, and it is then that the most

benefit is gained from light and shade and the clarity of the design. Think of the long low shadows from an orange winter sun cast by pencil cedars or a castellated hedge; a tremendously satisfying effect.

Other things to consider are the provision of privacy for the summer and of open spaces for children to play. They will need grass for the lively games of summer and a hard surface to avoid mud and damage in the winter. To get the most out of a garden, think of the luxury of a sitting area in a sun-trap, which could be comfortable on a sunny day in early spring or in autumn. Every detail has seasonal significance; if water features are included as part of the seasonal plan, then it is possible to have the sound of running water in the heat of summer and the still mirror-like surface of a pool to reflect scudding clouds in winter.

Far left: Bark like that of this red-stemmed dogwood (*Cornus alba*), can be an important feature of winter gardens. Many other trees and shrubs, especially birches, cherries and pines, have coloured bark that is a great bonus in winter.

Left: Most autumn foliage colours are complementary, as in the case of *Cotinus coggygria* 'Royal Purple' and *Acer palmatum.* There is no need to worry too much about colour schemes in this season, except to take into account possible clashes with highly valuable late season flowers.

Above: Fruits are just as much a part of the autumn scene as coloured leaves, so try to find room for some fruiting plants in your garden, even if it is on a wall. Here the rich tints of a medlar glow with seasonal promise. There is little to match the pleasure of harvesting home-grown fruit.

Right: This yellow border is infiltrated with golden-leafed evergreens, which will maintain colour and substance in the border long after the leaves on other plants have fallen. In summer they play a more discreet role.

COLOUR

As harmony is to a tune, so colour is to a garden: it gives a more precise feeling and mood to the underlying design. Colour alone cannot make a garden, but it can enrich the design and highlight different parts of the scheme at different times. It can attract attention by means of bright harmony or by shocking contrasts; it can produce tranquillity through quiet harmonies or monotones, or create movement within the design by means of flowing harmonies and contrasts (which is perhaps the most ambitious and difficult part of gardening). Edwardian herbaceous borders were so magnificent precisely because of their fine tuning of colour on a grand scale over a long season. Use colour purposefully, to your own ends and tastes, but never underestimate its power. Right and wrong may be in the eye of the beholder, but almost everyone recognizes chaos for what it is. Above all, colour in gardens is a means to an end like any other tool, rather than an end in itself.

Regardless of the effect sought through colour selection, there is no getting away from the need for green. It is the backbone of any colour scheme and should always be in evidence. There is a whole range to choose from: fresh apple greens will complement white and yellow, and warm bronzy greens will set off orange and scarlets. In a single-colour garden the presence of greens is particularly important and should be used to maximum effect.

Everything in a garden has colour, not just flowers, but foliage, walls, buildings, paths and seats. Together they offer the opportunity for endless experimentation and variety. If the hard landscaping has been inherited with the garden, the colour of brick walls, gravel and so on must be taken into account before embarking on a colour scheme to which they might be unsympathetic. A new site offers a rare opportunity: a chance to create the design, with the colours, of the gardener's dreams.

Left: Colour on its own cannot make a garden, but it is one of the most powerful instruments in the gardener's hand. It can shock, soothe or seduce; the gardener is in control.

Top left: Geranium × oxonianum 'Claridge Druce' under roses and border phlox contributes to a running variation on a theme of pink and mauve. A precise and limited colour scheme allows for subtle shifts of tone.

Bottom left: Foliage can be just as much a source of colour as flowers. Here, variegated hostas, meadowsweet, bamboo and golden catalpa form the basis of the colour scheme, while highlights of the same colour are provided by day lilies and helianthus.

Top right: Single-colour gardens are deservedly popular. Variety must come from shapes and textures rather than colour. Here, white 'Blizzard' tulips, grape hyacinths, forget-me-nots and pansies nestle beneath *Viburnum × carlcephalum*. It is the geometric rank of tulips which keeps the composition alive and anchors the display.

Bottom right: Some colours have to be used sparingly because they are so strong. In this detail the bright red of *Lychnis chalcedonica* is isolated in front of a delicate curtain of the cool grey weeping pear. Both plants benefit from the juxtaposition.

Above: The clashing colours of this vibrant, late-summer group of *Rudbeckia* and *Sedum*, with a tall background planting of asters, immediately attract the eye, thereby providing a lively focal point.

Although perception of colour and, certainly, taste is a personal and subjective matter, there are basic guidelines that can help you plan the colour schemes of your garden.

The theory behind colour combinations, both harmonies and contrasts, can be most readily understood by visualizing a chart known as the colour wheel. This is based on the colours of the spectrum and consists of the primary colours red, blue and yellow separated by the secondary, blended colours violet, green and orange. Colours adjacent to each other on the wheel, such as yellow and orange or blue and green, are generally considered to go well together, in other words they harmonize. Colours opposite each other, however, such as red and green or blue and orange, can be seen as contrasting colours, known as complementary colours.

There are, of course, infinite nuances of colour between each of these rather artificial subdivisions of the wheel. Colours can be pale or intense depending on the colours they are mixed with and, technically speaking, they become shades, tints and tones of the original base colour. A shade, for instance, is created by adding black to the base colour, while a tint is made by adding white, and a tone is the result of a colour being either lightened or darkened by the addition of grey.

Such variations make a huge difference to the effect of colour combinations; different intensities of one basic colour create a completely different feel. Take an apparently simple association of blue and yellow.

Far left: Juxtaposing complementary colours is always successful. In this flower bed, dark purple-blue *Lavendula* 'Hidcote Blue' makes an excellent foil for sharp, acid-yellow shades.

Left: Developing a one-colour theme is far from limiting, as this delightful border planting proves. From Lilium regale and Stachys at the front to the delphiniums at the back, this choice of plants shows great colour sensitivity.

Right: For a traditional herbaceous border, use strong contrasts of light and dark colour to produce a dynamic and stimulating effect. Here, the backdrop of dark foliage provided by the hedge shows the whites and pastel shades off to full advantage, while the intense shades of purple, pink and yellow create islands of colour that draw the eye along the length of the border.

Pale blue and pale yellow is a soft, unchallenging combination with a restful and airy feel to it. Now consider a mixture of golden yellow and violet blue and you have a far more vibrant and challenging effect which makes much more of a statement. However, both combinations have a place in the garden, the pale planting being particularly appropriate in a corner of an old walled garden for a timeless, relaxed atmosphere, and the stronger, lively scheme being perfect as part of a mixed planting along a path to promote the feeling of movement.

Colours can also be loosely divided into warm and cool effects, with greens and greys providing a neutral buffer zone in between. Reds, oranges and golden yellows seem warm, while purples and blues seem cooler. Furthermore, warm shades appear to advance towards the eye, making an area seem smaller than it really is, while cool colours seem to recede, thereby providing the illusion of space. In practise, if you clothe a garden in cool and light colours it will seem bigger than in reality, useful in small gardens, but, to make large gardens more intimate, you can interrupt a view and bring the eye up short with a strong display of bright, warm colours.

Experimenting with these effects is immensely enjoyable and the only way of developing your individual garden style. Don't be afraid of making mistakes, but it can be a good idea to try out colour combinations with bulbs or bedding plants first before investing time and money in the planting of shrubs and perennials.

Above: Even in the hot glare of summer sunlight this skilful combination of silvery-greys, pale yellows and soft mauves creates a cool, calming effect and makes the border seem larger.

Harmonizing Colours

Each of us sees colour differently, and one person's idea of bright harmonies may be another person's chamber of horrors. Nevertheless, there are certain basic guidelines which will help to produce harmonizing colours. Thereafter it is up to the individual to satisfy his or her tastes and to find the combinations that do most justice to the size, style and situation of a garden, a garden "room" or a flowerbed.

With colour, almost more than any other element in garden design, economy is the key. A few colours used carefully will be far more effective than a fussy mixture. Too many colours, used indiscriminately, will tend to cancel each other out and look either muddled, frantic or simply unattractive.

Colour harmonies can be made by several means. The simplest way is to use several varieties and tones of one colour, plus greens of course. This can be fun, but it is rather limited. Alternatively, one main colour can be combined with closely related colours – think of late summer borders of scarlet, oranges and browns or those intriguing mixtures of steely blue and grey foliage spiked with flowers of white and midnight blue. Another way, which is perhaps the hardest, is to

Above: On the colour wheel, blue and grey are neighbours and offset each other well. Grey is accommodating and will act as a foil for many other colours.

Above right: Blue and gold are contrasting colours, but can be made harmonious by using one in a pale form and one in a dark form. Here the rich blue of *Geranium himalayense* is combined with the paler blue of *Veronica gentianoides* and the soft yellow leaves and heads of Bowles' golden grass (*Milium effusum aureum*).

Below left: Different tones of one colour make a harmonious combination. Here, yellow is the dominant theme leading through the border, from *Achillea* 'Moonshine' on the left, through golden-leaved shrubs and trees, to *Rosa* 'Golden Wings' on the right.

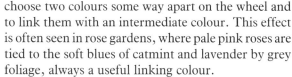

choose two colours some way apart on the wheel and to link them with an intermediate colour. This effect is often seen in rose gardens, where pale pink roses are tied to the soft blues of catmint and lavender by grey foliage, always a useful linking colour.

Colour harmonies can also be used to allow a large part of the spectrum to appear in one garden, by progressing from cool creams and yellows through warmer reds and oranges to purples and blues. Along the way it is possible to make a whole range of small contrasts and variations depending on taste and space, but the general progression will remain the same.

Colour relationships work not only through their relative positions in the spectrum but also through the strength and amount of colour used. A good guide is to have one or at most two colours that are dominant in strength but not in area, with other colours supporting in decreasing ranks.

Never forget the importance of green. It is often spoken of as if it were one colour, overlooking the fact that there is a whole range of different shades which can be just as useful in creating harmonies as any other colour which has a range of tones.

Below: Blue and red make a bold contrast, but here they are drawn together by intermediate colours such as pink, lavender and mauve. Using intermediate colours allows the creation of schemes that pass through several strong colours; if the design is well paced the effect can be wonderful. Gertrude Jekyll used intermediate colours in this way in her grand Edwardian flower borders.

Below right: Strong colours need to be used sparingly, as the culmination or highlight of a colour scheme. Here, deep red azaleas form a dense and dark base, leading upwards into lighter-textured pale pink, and finally into the airy, white structure of a magnolia tree. Strong colours used in tiny flashes have a very different, less startling effect than dense blocks of colour which hide every leaf.

One-colour Gardens

These have become popular in recent years in the wake of such famous examples as the white garden at Sissinghurst. They represent an extremely disciplined form of gardening in that the gardener has to work with a very limited palette. This can have its advantages: the emphasis is thrown back on to the elements of shape and texture, which is never a bad thing, and it suits small gardens because the simple and economic use of colour saves them from the clutter trap of having too many colours squeezed into a limited space. Larger gardens may use the single colour theme in just one small area, and in a garden where colour is used in an extravagant and complicated way this can come as a moment of relief from the hurly-burly. This is certainly true with a white garden which seems so clean and neutral to an eye that has been romping through the whole spectrum. Above all others, a white garden allows the viewer to appreciate the forms of the plants and the flowers: by removing the element of strong colour, the white palette gives a unique clarity to a planting scheme.

Single-colour gardening can be based on any colour – red, yellow, grey, blue, brown have all been used, as have black and white. Parallel herbaceous borders have been divided up into single colour sections facing each other across a path. Whichever colour is chosen, three things will remain paramount: the need for many shades of the chosen colour, the occasional contrasting colour, and the liberal use of greens throughout the garden or bed.

Above: In the famous "White Garden" at Sissinghurst grey and green are used as foils. The very formal design gives substance to the garden in winter, and there is much underplanting of bulbs to extend the season.

Left: Rosa rugosa 'Blanche Double de Coubert' has a relatively brief flowering period but it makes a delightfully cool combination with snow-in-summer (*Cerastium tomentosum*).

Right: Roses, pinks and peonies make a scrum of compatible pinks. The hard landscaping of steps and verandah, rather than contrasting foliage, provides the structure.

Even within a single colour there are many variations and degrees of density with which to make contrasts. A blue garden will almost certainly be improved if it contains the gamut of blues, from the midnight purple of *Salvia × superba* through the royal blue of agapanthus to the lavender and palest amethyst of violas and crocuses. It may contain more grey and silver foliage than green, but the overall effect will be a fanfare of blueness. There is no reason why a blue garden should not contain the occasional splash of another colour. Nature may do it for you, just as the dense blue-grey of rue will always throw up its crop of yellow flowers. The occasional splash of white will never seem out of place in a blue garden, while a steely autumn picture of juniper, rue, *Euphorbia characias wulfenii* and santolina can be enhanced by a streak of screaming pink schizostylis (kaffir lily). Select harmonious or contrasting colours to suit the mood.

Top right: Experimentation is needed when finding different shades of a colour to put together. Scarlet and pink are not automatically comfortable bedfellows, but with the chaperones of rich greens and plentiful greys to keep them apart, the effect is one of warm harmony and unity.

Right: There is no need to take too strict an approach to single-colour gardens. A little latitude will positively improve the look of a scheme, provided the principal colour (and therefore mood) remain dominant. Here, an array of blue, white and mauve delphiniums combine perfectly to produce an effect that is more than just an exercise in monochrome.

All-green Gardens

From time to time most gardeners long for an all-green garden. It is a longing for clarity and simplicity, for a rest from the business of gardening. The inspiration may be found in a formal garden: picture a white-painted weatherboard house with a long verandah overlooking still trees and emerald lawns striped with the shadows of beautifully clipped hedges. Or a more intensively planted garden may appeal, perhaps a dappled grove carpeted with choice woodland plants. Whatever the inspiration, an all-green garden is almost certain to be restful and easy on the eye. There is an easy-going naturalness about green gardens, even when made in a formal style.

Green gardens happily lean toward formality because in the absence of other colours they are free to fall back on the elements of texture and design. Some of the most striking green gardens are exclusively topiary gardens, which can be breathtaking displays of trained and tailored evergreens.

In a less formal context there is a huge range of all-green plants to choose from; plants, that is, which have green flowers as well as green foliage. Look at all the different greens in a flowering plant of *Euphorbia amygdaloides robbiae* or *Alchemilla mollis;* there is everything from dark green to pale grey-green and lime. A good green garden can incorporate every shade; emerald, olive and khaki all have their uses.

A green garden is a way of making the most of the simplest palette on offer, but it will also benefit from other discreet colours such as brown. There are brown, black and green barks to be had, and there is the russet and silver indumentum underneath the

Left: A green garden can throw the emphasis back onto the line, colour and texture of nearby buildings and paths. Here it highlights the configurations of the brickwork, the gateway and the floating forms of the "lollipop" bay trees. A shady courtyard is made into a delightful haven by this cool, formal approach.

leaves of some species of rhododendron. Grey foliage is not always sucessful in a green garden, as most grey-leaved plants are sun lovers and come from more naturally colourful plant communities.

Do not banish colour from a green garden. As with any single-colour garden, a little of the colour's close relatives (yellow and blue) can be incorporated with good effect. White also blends in very comfortably with green. *Tiarella*, *Aruncus*, Solomon's seal and primroses all offer a gentle touch of colour without moving away from that green-upon-green woodland feel. For the palest pinks, add Tellimas or dicentras.

Variegated foliage has a place in a green garden, but can by contrast look very artificial when surrounded by simple greens. It should be used sparingly. Most variegated foliage shows its best colours in full light and tends not to be successful in shady gardens. Slight shade is less of a problem to these plants and a dull corner will benefit from bright variegations.

Far left: Any one-colour garden is always improved by a touch of another colour. White or pale blue are the most discreet and perhaps best additions to green, as they enhance the feeling of purity and simplicity. Green itself has a whole range of tones, from the yellows of box and spiraea, as here, to sea greens, greys and blues. A mostly green garden is relaxing compared to an over-fussy floral display.

Left: Clipped shapes within the hedges echo the forms beyond: box spirals and tall conifers, box balls and stone balls, spiky phormium leaves and complementary patterns in the pathway.

Above: Variegated foliage has a most useful role to play in green gardens. It can add variety and provides a means of highlighting certain shapes and areas. Ivy and euonymus can be particularly useful.

Contrasting Colours

The colour wheel shows how the principal contrasts in colour are made – red with green, blue with orange and yellow with purple – but countless bold combinations can be used. These are strong effects, highlights to be used in garden design in a similar way to harmonies, but more sparingly. If a garden is overloaded with severe contrasts they cease to be effective. For instance, a golden-leaved conifer can make a brilliant highlight in the all-green days of winter, but plant a dozen of them and the effect is devalued.

A variety of smaller contrasts, in colour as in texture, are the stuff of interesting gardening. They keep the eye entertained and moving along. Sharp contrasts, like purple hazel next to yellow elder or a blue spruce with a yellow cypress, can draw attention and focus a garden, but they also hold up the progress of the eye, whereas smaller, gentler contrasts allow the eye to flow along. Indeed, the most harmonious of planting schemes will need a little contrast to keep it

Below left: Red has the ability to make green, its opposite on the colour wheel, all the more intense. Here, one form of the excellent, vibrant climber parthenocissus changes colour after another form, the autumn contrast being used to emphasize the line of the wall.

Above: Strong colours can have strong effects. This deep scarlet rose contrasts just as much with blue as it does with shell pink, when all colours are delivered in the same volume. The tiered effect – blue rising to red, rising to pink – is satisfying and clear.

alive and add that certain spark of the unexpected. A garden without enough contrast becomes a dull affair.

Colours which at full strength would war with one another can make good companions when one of them is used in a paler tint. The strong, creamy yellow of *Anthemis* 'Wargrave' would look crude beside royal blue delphiniums, yet if the misty lavender of *Thalictrum delavayi* were to be substituted for the delphinium there would be an interesting contrast, and the speck of yellow in the heart of the thalictrum flower would tie the two colours together. For a more gradual contrast, the thalictrum could be placed between the anthemis and the delphinium.

Contrast of foliage colour can be just as telling as that of flower colour, and this should be borne in mind when planning a garden. Schemes which are

Above: In a largely yellow colour scheme, a contained touch of deep maroon presents a strong highlight and focus that emphasizes the different lighter shades. The maroon is made more intense by the contrast, and the yellow is saved from being uneventful.

Below right: Contrasts of colour can be heightened by simultaneous contrasts of form. The solid green bulk of yew here acts as a foil to the light shape and texture of the airy lemon *Euphorbia characias wulfenii.* White blossom adds another subtle note.

intended to carry a great deal of bright flower colour will not require so much contrast or variety in the foliage: a reliable matrix of good stable greens will provide the best platform for floral pyrotechnics. By contrast, a garden which relies more on permanent shrubby plantings and evergreens will benefit from a greater range of contrasts in foliage colour.

Colour contrast can be made part of the whole garden design with certain areas set aside for strong hot colours, in direct contrast to other pale, cooler areas. These colour pools need not be kept separate in enclosed areas of the garden; instead, contrast can be used to enhance and distinguish the different sides of a more open prospect.

Remember that the effects made by colour depend upon the light in which they are seen. A really startling contrast may be devalued by siting it in shade, but, conversely, this effect can be used to temper an unwanted, unavoidable clash of colours.

Left: A gentle colour scheme of mauve and lemon can be given a sparkle by the addition of some rich blue and bright yellow, forming a greater contrast on the fringe. Grey helps to tie together the lemon and mauve. This late summer border gives a good impression of the flower and foliage effects that can be achieved with a planting of perennials and annuals. The main emphasis falls on the yellow *Achillea taygetea* and *Helichrysum* 'Sulphur Light', with their respectively flat and clustered flower heads and texturally interesting foliage. A campanula, to the right, gives height, while the delightful floriferous annual, *Xeranthemum annuum*, fills the foreground. Although it is drawing to the end of the growing season, the plants remain attractive. Fading flowers and mature foliage can have their own charm – subtlety compared to the vividness of high summer extravagance. The whole makes an enchanting scene. Notice the discreet supports around the rose bushes at either side.

TEXTURES

Texture works with shape and colour in a garden to create movement and harmony for the eye. In contrast with themselves and each other, these three elements produce a constantly changing variety of interest, bringing the detail of the garden to life. The greater range of textures, the greater will be the interest throughout the space.

It is easy to forget that everything in a garden has its own texture; not only are there the textures of foliage, grass, flowers and bark, but also those of water, paths, walls, gravel and all the other areas of hard landscaping. Texture is a more discreet element than colour or shape, and a wide range of textures will not clutter a garden so much as highlight its other elements. So it is worth trying to incorporate plenty of different textures in all aspects of the garden.

We are made aware of texture in different ways; partly through direct sight and touch – we can see and feel if a leaf is rough and hairy – and partly through the way light falls on surfaces – we expect shiny rhododendron leaves to be smooth and firm or a glistening, wet stone-flagged path to be harder than gravel. This indirect visual appreciation of texture needs to be part of the planning of texture in a garden as much as the tactile element.

Hard landscape features can be softened by the use of textures. Consider the use of "green" steps, where the risers are planted with ivy or some tiny cotoneaster; think of deep cobbles or precise herringbone bricks with emerald green moss in every joint. The features themselves also offer a wide range of textures, from hard concrete to fine footstep-deadening grit. In a precise, formal garden, where much of the design is dictated by architectural features, large quantities of polished marble can look perfect on walls or underfoot, most usually in the form of a well-proportioned staircase. By contrast, in a minimalist style, where incidental details are more appropriate

Above: Texture and form work hand in hand. Here, smooth circles of hard and rugged paving contrast with the brittle hard lines of yuccas and the architectural, blue-grey Atlas cedar. The domes of golden yew are soft in detail and texture but have a hard form when clipped.

Above: Textural contrasts need not be extreme to be effective. The roughness of this gravel is suitably offset by a gentle mixture of soft shapes and textures, seen in both the foliage and the adjacent surfaces. The delicate, mounding Japanese maple rightfully takes centre stage.

Left: The tall Chusan palm has its own internal contrast of textures. Hard, flapping leaves stand above a rugged hairy stem. A woodland floor, rippling with bluebells, complements the softness of the trunks to produce a calm, gentle aspect. Although the tree is distinctly exotic in appearance it is frost hardy. It does, however, need full sun, fertile, well-drained soil and shelter from strong winds.

Above: Texture can be a matter of scale. Here the spiky flowers of the dwarf laurel *Prunus laurocerasus* 'Otto Luyken' combine *en masse* to form a soft carpet of green and white. As a contrast, the light glossy texture of box is clipped into a hard wheel shape to be doubly effective. Colour and form underline the textural contrast. The whole effect shows the highly original nature of garden design.

than clearly delineated patterns, a great river-washed boulder will combine a gentle shape with a hard texture without imposing uncompromising order.

The range of textures to be found in foliage is immense, but they can reasonably be grouped into the following categories: feathery, soft, felty or hairy, rugged, spiky, hard, smooth or shiny.

Feathery leaves make you instantly want to touch them. Some, like fennel and ladslove, release a perfume when touched. There are the green or purple domes of the dwarf maple, *Acer palmatum dissectum*, the tougher birch 'Trost's Dwarf' or the fern-leaved elder. There is the billowy foliage of 'Boulevard' cypresses, the brittle delicacy of dicentras or the flowers themselves of the smoke bush, *Cotinus coggygria*, which is smothered in panicles of wonderful, fluffy blossoms during summer.

Softness comes in many guises, from the swaying fountains of bamboos and ornamental grasses to the simple eloquence of moss. Ferns offer some deliciously soft textures over a long season. Meadow grass rippling in the wind must surely be one of the garden's most seductive softnesses, while in a border plants like *Alchemilla mollis* will act as a gentle foil for more vigorous shapes.

Feltiness or hairiness is often to be found on large leaves, like those of *Hydrangea sargentiana* and *Bergenia ciliata*, or on the undersides of some species rhododendron leaves which can have a rich indumentum of grey or russet. Lambs' ears (*Stachys byzantina*) is a favourite with children, and many people like to stroke the cerise velvet flowers of *Salvia buchananii*.

Ruggedness shows up well in the striking corrugated leaves of veratrums, rodgersias, *Viburnum davidii* and

V. rhytidophyllum, and the vast umbrella leaves of *Gunnera manicata*. There are barks too, flaky, deeply corrugated, striped, or even peeling in shreds and tatters.

Spikiness appears most often in the sword-like foliage of irises, crocosmias, phormium and yucca, and in the prickles of holly and eryngiums. Acanthus, morina and eryngiums also have spiny flowers.

Hard textures are found in shiny broad-leaved and needle-bearing evergreens, in the rigidity of yuccas and in the tight surfaces of topiary and cushion plants like *Bolax* or *Hebe* 'Boughton Dome' (which is as crusty-looking as a new cottage loaf).

Glossy leaves grace evergreen shrubs like laurel, aucuba and griselinia, but there is just as much shine on the foliage of herbaceous plants like galax or asarum. Remember that some barks can be shiny too, especially some species of cherry and birch.

Opposite: Amid a generalized soft planting of ferns and primulas, the striking textures come from the shiny surface of the water and the rugged bark of the silver birch. These elements together produce a balanced effect.

Top left: In a planting of soft shapes and textures, the hard lines of stepping stones can be used to give clarity to the structure of the garden.

Top right: The combinations of texture and form can vary greatly. The shape of this pampas grass is undeniably stiff, yet the flower plumes are soft and yielding. The dome of 'Jackman's Blue' rue has a broad, draping form that matches its soft texture.

Bottom left: Texture is often deceptive. The purple euphorbia is far softer than the surrounding cotoneaster branches, yet their geometric structure would lead you to expect them both to be hard. Greater contrast of form would benefit these textures.

Bottom right: The leaves of this purple cordyline and the surrounding griselinia are equally hard, yet the contrast of form is extreme.

GARDEN
STYLES

STYLES

The style of a garden is largely responsible for its atmosphere, whether it is neat and geometric, relaxed and informal, busy and colourful, or still and discreet. The choice of style is often influenced by other gardens that have been seen and admired. Try to be open-minded about the styles you look at, and consider not just their personal appeal, but also how they would suit your house and family use, and how much maintenance they would create and when. Styles which rely on a very detailed planting to look correct will require a great deal of summer attention which you may not be able to give. On the other hand, a style which is architecturally complex may be more expensive to construct but far easier to maintain during the growing season. Some of the great historic garden styles have been extremely simple in terms of plant material, relying more on the form of the land, on water and buildings, and such staples as grass and trees. This restrained approach can produce stunning results, whatever the scale of the site. Let period styles be a source of inspiration, a starting point rather than something to copy slavishly. It is too easy to let period style become a cliché: draw the best from it and make it your own. After all, every style was modern once. By giving serious consideration at the outset to style, ideas are often enriched and crystallized and the temptation to simply fill the garden with a mass of favourite plants avoided.

Left top and bottom: Classical formality or cottage garden? You must decide what suits your house, your household (children and pets as well as adults) and your pocket. It is also important to consider how much time you are prepared to put into gardening and the length of time you are likely to stay before moving. Choosing the right style will maximize the pleasure you receive.

Above left: Select a design appropriate to your interests. The clear lines of a modern designer garden can be obscured by rich planting so may not suit the plant lover.

Above right: With care, you can make your own style by mixing unlikely elements. The combination of classical urn, cottagey pots and modern paving works as a satisfying composition of shapes and colour. The attention given to the paved design allows other details to be simpler.

Below: If time and money are plentiful, the Victorian style may be for you. But would you always want a garden so rich in detail in all its parts, so formal, so ostentatiously gardened? Might you prefer a simpler, classical approach to formality, that gives order to a space without such abundance?

Water

Water is potentially one of the most important, effective and varied elements in garden design. Not only does it provide the ideal opportunity to experiment with aquatic and moisture-loving plants, but it introduces a new texture to the garden and, in the case of moving water, something no other garden feature provides: sound.

The great gardens of the past show a masterly understanding of water. The enticing fountain gardens of the Alhambra in Spain, with their play of light and shade, concealment and revelation, represent one of the most subtle and successful uses of water. By contrast, more grandiose features such as those at Versailles in France or the Villa d'Este in Italy show just how elaborate the presence of water can be. For domestic use, however, water is not always that easy to introduce. At its best, when handled subtly and appropriately placed, any water feature can lend a magical quality to the garden, but when it appears gratuitous, over-elaborate or just plain ugly, it will only detract from what could have been a perfectly acceptable garden scene. As far as water goes, restraint and planning are the key.

Below: The delicate spray of this fountain acts as a foil to the colourful, abundant planting of roses behind.

Right: An impressive, large-scale cascade form a dramatic focal point in a large, steeply sloping garden.

Above: This small, shallow pool is defined by a selection of carefully placed pebbles and stones that make the water accessible to birds and animals.Colour is provided by the white flowers and greenery of a simple planting of arums.

Water features must, of course, be planned on a scale in proportion with your house and garden. Obviously there is more scope for different types of features in a large garden than in a small one but, as a general rule, water close to the house tends to look best if kept fairly formal, while further away more natural-looking schemes can be integrated into the landscape. To maximize the mirror-like effect of a formal pond, it should be sited so as to reflect as much light as possible, whereas informal pools should blend into the surrounding garden, and the addition of a bog garden can often help to do this. Movement can be created in many ways, as simple or as complex as you like or can afford; mill stones or piles of well-rounded pebbles surrounding bubbles of water are easy to install and, importantly, present no risk to children, unlike deeper water features. A small basin fed by a trickling spout is another safe choice. If space and budget permit, fountains of all shapes and sizes are an exciting option, forming different patterns of light and evocative sounds that will draw any visitor inexorably towards them.

Unless you are lucky enough to have a natural water feature running through your garden, installing water is bound to involve some degree of construction work. This could take the form of earth moving and excavation for sunken features or building and brickwork for raised ponds and pools. Try and think through all the necessary stages of construction before starting work.

Left: This soft, informal planting of primulas and irises within a strictly symmetrical framework is a perfect feature for a small garden. The water channel leads to a small, brick-lined pool, which provides a delightful focal point at the edge of a crisp, well-tended lawn.

Right: This well-established pool achieves a balance between the formality of its shape and statuary and the relaxed planting style. Ferns, mosses and sedums have been allowed to colonize the gaps in the surrounding paving, while irises and water lilies provide interest in the water.

Below: Few gardeners are lucky enough to have a natural river bank to cultivate, but this example has been planted up with a selection of shrubs and perennials, including *Phormium, Senecio* and *Sedum.* All these garden subjects are suited to the rather dry raised ground around the paved area.

Right: Even the smallest garden can have a water feature. Despite its tiny size, this sunken tub has been planted with a variety of carefully chosen water plants. Although maintenance will be minimal, the tub must be regularly cleaned and tended to ensure a healthy balance in the plant life.

Far right: A classic pairing of irises and water lilies provides the main interest in this colourful aquatic planting. The flagged surround, softened with mounds of natural-looking plants, is practical in that it allows easy access to the pond.

Wild

Most gardeners understand what is meant by a wild garden even though it is really a contradiction in terms. How can a garden, a man-made creation, be truly wild? The main characteristic is that nature is apparently allowed to have the upper hand over the gardener, but in a successful wild garden this is never actually so. The gardener produces this illusion by keeping maintenance to a discreet minimum and by choosing plants which will not take advantage of this kind of freedom. It is a quiet lyrical style of gardening, a balance between the truly natural and the contrived which is surprisingly difficult to achieve.

The fashion for a more relaxed approach to gardening first appeared in the late seventeenth century, when large gardens often included a "wilderness": an intersecting network of paths and vistas running between areas of trees and shrubs, and sometimes hedges. This was wild only in that it contrasted with the more rigidly formal gardens nearer the house. Wild gardening as we know it today was pioneered in the late nineteenth century by the writer William Robinson as a reaction to the ostentatious formality of the high Victorian period. In *The Wild Garden* (1870) he advocated naturalizing "perfectly hardy exotic plants under conditions where they will thrive without further care". It was he who first persuaded the hybrid daffodil out of the bed and into the long grass; yet even he was content to have areas of more closely managed formality around the house.

Today, the notion of wild gardening has become associated with the idea of nature conservation, and one hears more of putting back native plants than

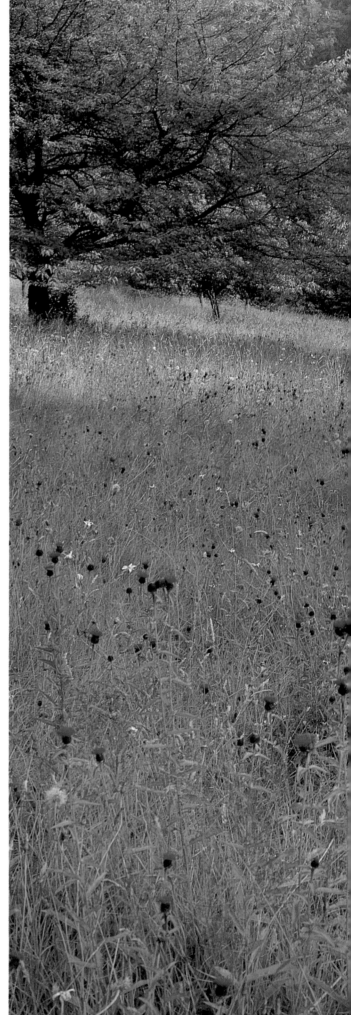

Far left: Naturalized bulbs, like these anemones and small early daffodils, are perfect for creating decorative drifts of colour in a wild garden. The grass here would not be cut until mid-summer, allowing the foliage of the naturalized plants time to feed the bulbs and die down first. Wild daffodils self-seed readily in these conditions.

introducing foreign ones. We have become aware of gardens as living communities, not just of plants but also of birds, animals like hedgehogs and squirrels, insects, fungi, and even lichens.

Certain rules of thumb are worth remembering when creating a wild garden. First, the garden needs to be big enough to have its own identity to avoid looking like a small shabby part of an otherwise well maintained garden. It may be advantageous to separate the wild area visually from the rest of the garden. Second, it is usually more appropriate to keep wild gardening at some distance from the house. Close contrast with a neat house will make a wild garden look muddled rather than relaxed and comfortable.

The wild garden should be planned for minimum maintenance. Lawns may even become flower meadows, cut as hay in late summer, with paths mown through them for access. Safe old trees should be left to decline gracefully and woodland plants should be cultivated beneath them. Use plenty of bulbs and shrubs which can compete with grass and require next to no pruning or spraying. It may be a good idea to introduce a pond if the time is available to maintain it. Above all, do not overplant: nature is an economical gardener and gains her best effects very simply, with just a few plants.

Left: A wild-flower meadow makes a superb transitional zone between garden and country. Wild gardening, when it is successful, can be sheer magic.

Below: In damp woodland, primulas, ferns, bluebells and forget-me-nots multiply. Such a display needs weeding in spring but later in the year requires minimal attention.

Left: This early summer scene has a wonderfully fresh and relaxed quality. Vigorous roses look well in turf, and can be allowed to sprawl freely. Try to choose mildew-resistant varieties, and then leave them.

Below left: Much of wild gardening is a matter of keeping the peace. Having established wild flowers where you want them, the general maintenance regime should allow them to increase freely, apart from the most vigorous.

Below right: An informal pond cannot be beaten for imparting that wild look, even when, as here, exotic plants are combined with native ones. Ponds also provide a habitat for wildlife, including fish, amphibians, insects and certain birds.

Right: A simple hazel-nut walk can be transformed into a garden with a minimum of planting. Self-seeding bluebells are given that little extra spark by the addition of a few scarlet tulips.

Below left: Wild gardening should be simple, but can still be subtle. Here, native foxgloves and the wild *Rhododendron ponticum* make a perfect early-summer combination alongside a soft path. Purples can be all the more opulent in shade.

Below right: Wild flowers may often be small, but *en masse* they are just as effective as larger garden flowers, if a little less precise. These buttercups contribute just as much to this scene as the pink pokers of the cultivated bistort.

Topiary

Despite the vituperations of those who regarded topiary as "pastry cooks' gardening", it has always had a loving following somewhere. Whatever topiary might do for the style of a garden, there is always pleasure to be taken in the sheer craftsmanship of creating and maintaining it. In manageable quantities, making topiary is fun.

The clipping of yew, holly and box played an important part in seventeenth-century gardens and came to the fore again in the grand formal gardens of the high Victorian era. Large gardens of the twentieth century have often made bold use of topiary, and it has long been a part of the cottage garden tradition.

The continuing appeal of topiary stems from the fact that it is an effective (and also inexpensive) means of creating the structure of a garden. A fine hedge with knife-edged finials marching on top is every bit as much a part of the garden's structure and ornament as a stone wall would be. A well-placed and freestanding topiary specimen, in whatever style, will command just as much dramatic attention as a fine statue.

Topiary is essentially a formal style of gardening. It is the imposition of the gardener's will upon the plant, a living sculpture. This degree of artificiality immediately commands the onlooker's attention and makes competition from mere flowers seem rather petty. Consequently, topiary is best used where it has the space to be seen on its own terms. The faintly comical mixture of topiary and a gentle jumble of flowers in cottage gardens is perhaps why topiary there has tended to be humorous in inspiration.

Whole gardens of topiary are best kept simple. The point of concentration should be in the contrast of curves and straight lines, of light and shadow, of earthbound or floating forms. A lawn or clean gravel is all that is needed to set off these living sculptures, but you can extend the interest by adding a little coloured foliage such as golden yew, or some simple washes of colour provided by bedding plants.

Topiary is not in itself a labour-intensive craft. Only the amount of topiary you have will make it a chore, especially if ladders are needed. Patience and skill are the keys. Once the shapes are fully formed, an annual clipping is sufficient for yew and box, carried out at the gardener's convenience during autumn or early winter. Topiary can be made out of holly and bay too, but there is no doubt that yew is much the best. Good topiary is slow to take shape, which is why so many topiary gardens conveniently begin life with a more diverse planting until the topiary develops its own singular authority.

Left: This great topiary cartwheel is almost a garden in itself. It is made entirely of box, both the green and yellow forms, giving structural contrast throughout the year. Interplanting is restrained.

Below: Strong, towering forms produce a maze-like effect, which offers new vistas at every turn. A bold structure like this can cope with a loose, informal underplanting.

Above: Single-colour bedding emphasizes the geometric design in this scheme of great clarity and simplicity. There is contrast in the hard paths and the play of sunlight on the imaginative shapes.

Top left: These three-sided pyramids of yew make a wonderful abstract sculpture. They would be difficult to maintain without the use of a small scaffold: very tall topiary specimens always present difficulties of this kind.

Top right: Box bushes will respond well to hard pruning. This old specimen has been cut back to its framework of branches and the new growth has been cloud-pruned to form a clever vegetable poodle of considerable charm.

Below: Spiral box sentinels of this size require many years of skilful training on a wire frame. Specimens that have already been trained are expensive: weigh your means against your patience.

Left: A living chessboard of topiary makes a magnificent conversation piece. Note the contrast of straight and curved lines. Irish yew (on the perimeter) is too weak to make good upright cylinders and always leans. Purple and grey always complement topiary.

Top left and right: The precise hedging of a parterre or knot garden is just as hard to maintain well as more fanciful pieces of topiary. In topiary it is always the straight lines that take time to perfect. The job is made easier if a stretched line is used as a cutting guide.

Below: Yew can be shaped more tightly than any other tree or shrub that is suitable for topiary. These flattened balls look as hard as the winter frost upon them.

Town

Town gardens have much to offer and provide an exciting, if challenging, opportunity to produce many an interesting and original garden design. A little forward planning and careful thought can go a long way towards overcoming any immediate problems such as lack of direct sunlight, shadows cast from neighbouring buildings, poor soil or pollution.

Generally speaking, town gardens are easier and cheaper to maintain than most country gardens simply because they are usually smaller. Urban sites also tend to be more sheltered than rural ones and may even be frost-free as well, enabling a wide range of

tender plants to be grown without protection. Furthermore, unpleasant though it may be, sulphur-based air-pollution makes fungus diseases less prevalent; indeed, some city rose bushes are never affected by blackspot or mildew.

Formal rather than informal designs tend to be more popular for town gardens because it is easier to incorporate surrounding party walls into a methodical, precise concept. When choosing your design, remember that the garden will be seen as much from the upper storeys of the house as the lower and, as a general rule, formal rather than informal designs tend to look better from above.

Size is seen as one of the most common limitations of town gardens, but there are plenty of design options that can be employed to help deceive the eye. Small plots can be made to seem bigger by the use of different levels linked by steps and, for floor treatment, diagonal or circular paving is space enhancing.

Far left: Here, a well-planted archway is used as a screening device to break up one large rectangular area into two smaller ones.

Left: This dense, informal urban planting, which includes plenty of evergreens as well as flowering subjects, will appeal all year round for maximum seasonal interest.

Below: Surrounding buildings provide shelter but tend to throw shadows across gardens. White flowers can be used to brighten up gloomy areas.

A series of hidden areas linked by a winding path can give the illusion of space. The careful use of *trompe l'oeil* (a painting or decoration that creates an illusion, tricking the viewer into seeing something that is not really there) is another useful device for creating a false sense of space. Wall plants and climbers also play a vital role because they increase the surface area of the garden vertically rather than horizontally. As an added attraction, a plant-clad wall or fence will provide a degree of privacy.

Lack of light is another constraint often encountered in town gardens, and the only option here is to select shade-tolerant plants. There are many exciting ones to choose from, however, and a careful mixture of foliage and flowering plants will bring much colour and interest. For those gardens surrounded by walls, it is possible to paint one or all of the walls white to reflect any light the garden receives. Excessively dry sites are also common and are among the most taxing to work with, but there are plenty of plants tolerant of such extreme conditions. Containers and hanging baskets can be used to make up for poor soil in the rest of the garden, and they can also be employed as a means of providing more planting space for a series of seasonal displays.

This approach of choosing plants that positively relish the prevailing situation and making the most of the available light, water and space epitomizes town gardening at its best.

Above: The successful use of strong geometry in this plan is particularly evident when it is viewed from upstairs. Emphasising the diagonal and establishing a dense planting of wall climbers draws attention away from the regular shape of the garden.

Left: The design of some gardens is based on the sinuous curves of its borders. Here, they are planted with a good mixture of evergreen and deciduous trees and shrubs, which focus attention within the confines of the garden so what is outside scarcely impinges at all. Well-tended perennials and half hardy annuals, chosen for shade tolerance, add interest at a lower level.

Below: Front gardens are permanently on display and so are best kept simple and neat. This highly formal design has the additional advantage of requiring minimal upkeep. The hedges and cones are box, which needs to be trimmed only once a year, although twice yearly would give a neater outline. The fact that it is slow growing does mean that it can take several years to form satisfactory shapes. The decorative gravel mulch is also labour-saving.

Right: A densely planted patio provides an oasis of calm in a town garden. Although the ivy and other wall plants, once established, will largely look after themselves, plants in unglazed terracotta pots need very regular watering.

Bottom: Creating a pond, whatever size, really adds an extra dimension to a town garden. This ambitious design includes raised decking, wooden walkways and a lush, rather exotic planting.

Cottage

The best words to sum up the cottage garden style might be unpretentious or unsophisticated. It is a style in which a random variety of plants is grown, not particularly for the subtleties of careful plant association but simply as favourites, because they are loved for their own sake or are useful in some way. The garden in which they grow will have a small-scale, purely functional framework, without any grand vistas or extravagant hard landscaping. This is because a cottage garden is essentially an elaboration of a working

garden, a fruit and vegetable garden made pretty by flowers with the minimum of expense.

The cottage garden was developed by people who could not afford designer gardens, in the days when cottage meant a humble dwelling in a rural setting rather than a desirable small house in the country. So, for instance, paths were of simple local materials, no wider than absolutely necessary, and lay where necessity required – for instance, from the front door to the garden gate, from the front door round to the back door or from the back door to a garden shed. Gates were simply made, perhaps of painted wood rather than metal. A rustic fence or boundary hedge kept passing farm animals out and would have been of native plants such as holly and hawthorn, forming a transition from garden to country.

Pursuing the theme of a productive garden, in a modern cottage garden the trees should be fruit trees wherever possible, or at least blossom trees of some kind. Apples, pears, plums and cherries will all help

Left: In the soft light of
evening this cottage garden
seems to merge with the
countryside beyond, with the
fields seen through a screen of
old espalier apple trees and
roses trained over a rustic
arbour and fence. Free-
seeding has helped to produce
the relaxed plant groupings in
the foreground; it also quickly
gives a look of maturity.

to create the right atmosphere, as will nut trees such as hazel or almond. If there is space for a large tree, a walnut might do. Try to avoid large upright conifers. Evergreens such as holly or yew will look more appropriate and they can be clipped into shapes which add a touch of fun and formality to the garden if required. Lawns should not play an important part in a cottage garden. Open spaces suitable for lawns would in a real cottage garden be used for vegetables, so if you need grass for children grow it under fruit trees.

Colourful plants, or perhaps herbs, in simple pots by the door will look right. Make the most of vegetables and fruit bushes, letting them be part of the garden design. Do not be afraid of using rows of vegetables, herbs, bedding plants or flowers for cutting, especially alongside a path. There is no need to grow only old fashioned flowers because it is how the flowers are used and grouped that creates the cottage style not what type they are. Choose as many scented plants as can be fitted into the space available, especially climbing roses and honeysuckle.

The overall effect should be of fussy well-tended order, a comfortable mix in which all the plants are allowed to run together. There will be plenty of weeding, but also an opportunity to grow all your favourite plants in rich profusion.

Far left: Foxgloves, clematis and lovage grow freely in an informal border, backed by low, simple architecture that seems at one with nature.

Below: This arbour is engulfed by a luxuriant growth of mixed climbers; plants drape over the path, giving the scene an intimate mood.

Left, top right and centre right: In cottage gardening, the planting is visually more important than the structure. Paths can be overwhelmed with plants – just so long as you can get by – and the built structure of the garden should be made of simple materials. Smart, sophisticated materials look out of place. Local stone or brick are ideal materials for walls and paving. Rough-cut timber or rustic logs are most suitable for arches.

Bottom far left: Built features in a cottage garden should be well made but simple, like this wicket under a nut arch.

Bottom left: Topiary, often whimsically shaped, is a traditional feature of many cottage gardens.

Below: This excellent example of dry-stone walling shows high quality construction and the use of sympathetic materials. The pink hue in the stone complements the foxgloves. Simple furniture is entirely appropriate.

Bottom right: Showy wild flowers, like foxgloves and herbs, strike a suitably unpretentious note in a cottage garden. Lavender makes an attractive lining to paths, tempting passersby to pick it. Flowers for drying, like helichrysums, honesty and Chinese lanterns, fit in well.

Modern

It is ironic to think that every historical garden style was once the latest thing, fresh and exciting. But what makes a garden modern today? Certainly not the plants themselves, for the world contains no more unexplored continents to offer us startling new introductions as it did during the last 400 years; and while we can reconstruct or draw inspiration from period styles to make something new, the result would not immediately be called a modern garden.

The most clearly modern tendency in gardening is to follow the leads of modern architecture and painting towards a minimalist style, using plenty of clean, modern hard landscaping materials and a much reduced palette of plants. The plants, such as grasses and bamboos, are often chosen more for their foliage and architectural qualities than for their flowers, because the modern style springs precisely from the contrast of shapes and textures between plant and plant, and between plant and hard landscaping.

Due to this predominance of hard landscaping, the modern style is especially suitable for town gardens and courtyards. Here sculpture can bring life to this kind of precise, discreet garden, and it looks more at home than in some traditional styles. Water can be used in mirror pools, trickling over pebbles or in fountains to bring light and movement to the design.

Below: Modern gardens tend to use few plants and there is an emphasis on line and hard landscaping. These pebble arabesques are unashamedly modern, yet are inspired by the parterres of earlier periods and the decorative style of Spanish and Moorish architecture. Could this open space happily stand further complication of its lines?

Left: High-quality materials, such as marble and slate, deserve the attention drawn to them in this angular garden. The fountain and the stylish, sweeping pergola add movement to the design.

Above: An "outdoor room", complete with tiled floor, cleverly uses the contrast between the rough texture of grass and the smooth texture of stone. The linear pattern lengthens the garden.

There are so many different modern paving materials that the possibilities for interesting effects are endless. Concrete paving slabs come in all sizes and colours, from simple rectangles to hexagons. Bricks offer a wonderful range of colours and opportunities for patterned textures. Wooden decking is increasingly used in warm dry climates as a means of surfacing outdoor areas, and it can easily accommodate sudden changes in level.

Another development of modern architecture has been the large plate glass window, which has helped to bring the garden into the house. Equally, everyone likes to have a living area outside in the garden, where the family can eat, read or amuse themselves when the weather permits. These two factors have combined to blur the distinction between indoors and outdoors. Swimming pools have further emphasized this ambiguity and have also introduced another form of hard landscaping into the garden, a feature that requires careful placing and design. Materials usually found indoors have come to be used outside, and it is not unusual to see ceramic tiles on the floor and walls of a patio, as well as in swimming pools. Where shade is needed for outdoor living, modern gardens have made use of specimen trees with ornamental bark set off by a gravel surround, so that the beauty of the trunk becomes a feature in itself.

It is in the modern garden that the curve, the organic shape, has found its proper home. Curved lawns, curved pools and curved paving marry in well with this flowing, informal style.

Above left: Unashamedly artificial curves are perfectly at home in the hard landscaping of a modern garden. The angular pattern of the paving only serves to accentuate the curves of the low retaining wall. Modern grey slabs and a sweep of old dark bricks are effectively juxtaposed.

Above: The modern style suits small courtyards and town gardens. In this example, the relationship to the house is enhanced by the use of quarry tiles on the steps; they give warmth to the scene and are probably seen from a vantage point inside the house as often as from the garden.

Left: The large simple shapes, made possible in modern architecture by the use of concrete, find a complement in natural forms: the spiny disks of cacti contrast splendidly with the smooth rectangles of paving. Gravel is a discreet foil to both.

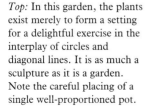

Top: In this garden, the plants exist merely to form a setting for a delightful exercise in the interplay of circles and diagonal lines. It is as much a sculpture as it is a garden. Note the careful placing of a single well-proportioned pot.

Bottom left: Sculptural foliage, water, and hard landscaping blend well together. The clever tunnel-stepping-stone contributes liveliness and a sense of direction to this carefully poised composition of mixed materials.

Bottom right: Here a rather ordinary back yard has been transformed into an attractive outdoor room. The emphasis is on gravel, paving and the wooden supports for the "roof", which gives a feeling of privacy and seclusion

without making the space dark. The pale gravel also helps to keep it light, as does the delicate statue on tip-toes. Modern gardens make a good setting for modern sculpture; a sympathetic environment can be made around it.

Victorian

The interiors of Victorian houses were known for their fussiness and crowding detail; so it was with the gardens of the high Victorian period. Labour was cheap and numerous gardeners could be employed, removing worries about whether a garden style might be labour intensive or not. The period was also marked by a passionate interest in scientific discovery and the cultivation of those plants which were being introduced from far-off countries. These two factors led Victorian gardening away from eighteenth-century debates on the aesthetics of design towards an interest in plants for their own sake, for their collecta-bility as specimens. The result was a style of garden-ing as formal and ostentatious as gardening has ever been. Everything was kept very dressy indeed.

Above: The Victorians loved to use formal vases, and to plant them up with striking specimens for the summer. Yuccas have been used here, to top off two already enormous vases that have been raised on pedestals to frame the hedges and the path. The Victorians were not in the least afraid to be a little pompous, or to gild the lily.

What the gardens of the great houses did one day, the villa gardens of the new suburbs did the next but on a smaller scale. Whereas in the eighteenth century country landowners had vied with each other for supremacy in good taste, the new one-upmanship was in the material contents and the sheer quantity of plants used in a garden.

Typical features of the period include close-shaven lawns, frequently changed bedding schemes, par-terres, extravagantly winding paths, iron pergolas and arches, cast iron seats, urns and balustrades, and

Below: Victorian gardens made the most of ironwork, and of roses. The elegant top of this gazebo and the swags of roses between its pillars make a fine wedding-cake feature.

the very generous use of specimen trees at the expense of open space. Conservatories, glasshouses and vegetable and fruit gardens were beautifully and precisely maintained. Formality was the keynote in all things, whether the garden was full of curves or straight lines. Nothing was discreet: all the work was for show.

Even specimen trees were clipped and evergreens such as holly and yew were used a great deal for the purpose. Weeping trees were especially favoured as specimens, not least of which was the weeping holly. Monkey puzzles sprouted on every lawn with a pretence to fashion. Evergreen shrubberies were common and made much use of three laurels: spotted laurel, Portugal laurel and cherry laurel, largely because they withstood the sooty Victorian town

Left: Grandeur in miniature was the keynote of Victorian villa gardens. Here there are terraces with imposing central steps, but all in rather light materials. The planting is used to emphasize the central axis, with pairs of clipped box and griselinia flanking the steps. The use of coloured gravel and rope-tile edging adds to the sense of order.

atmosphere so well. Roses were the great favourite and could be trained hard. Small, perfectly-edged island beds would be cut into lawns to house specimens such as a potted cabbage palm or a mass of red-hot pokers, surrounded by rings of brightly coloured annuals. Gravel paths were popular, kept perfectly clean and well raked with a rope-tile edging. Even tarmac came to be used for its precise looks. Urns were common and were planted rather than used as ornaments in themselves. In short, the Victorian style can offer some unforgettable eye-opening effects.

Above: Victorian gardens were places of entertainment and education, as much as havens of peace. Aviaries like this were common and were used to house collections of newly discovered, extraordinary birds. Conservatories housed exotic plants in a similar way.

Left: The Victorians loved formal fountains, especially when they were set in a large pool. With electric pumps and countless reproduction fountains, similar effects can readily be achieved today.

Below: Fashionable Victorian gardens never shied away from complicated features. Economy of design, or of labour, was not respected: in the great country houses of England, entire bedding schemes could be changed overnight, while weekend guests dined and slept.

Above: Roses, bedding, a planted urn and lots of white paint make a typically Victorian combination. The late nineteenth century saw a considerable fashion for the idea of charming cottage gardening and roses around the door. Here, a modern interpretation of picket fencing is successfully coupled with a chinoiserie bench (a style popular from the 1760s) and Victorian-style planting.

Top right: A box-edged parterre in Victorian style complements a good cast-iron seat and elaborate jardinière. Centrepieces like this were common in formal gardens. The contents could be changed regularly as plants came into flower under glass.

Bottom right: No lawn could be too well maintained for Victorian taste, so, if you have the patience, a fine lawn should be your aim. Specimen trees were used a great deal, including forest conifers and, of course, the monkey puzzle. Bedding was often used under the canopy of young specimen trees or on its own, in small, well planted island beds.

Parterre

A good parterre is about as stylized a piece of gardening as you will ever find. It turns the surface of the garden into a picture, a pattern complete in itself. In principle it is one of the simplest of garden styles, however complex the geometry of the pattern itself may actually be.

Knot gardens were a feature of seventeenth-century gardens and consisted of a square plot upon which lines of dwarf shrubs were interwoven to form a symmetrical pattern. The style developed, under French influence, into the parterres of the early eighteenth century. Here a larger area was divided with small hedges into all kinds of shapes, such as animals, crests, arabesques and leaves. The areas between the hedges were filled variously with grass, flowers, shrubs, or coloured substances such as gravel, fluorspar, sand, coal, crushed brick and glass. Clipped evergreens were also used, in pots or in the ground, to add a further dimension to the patterns. Much later, in the mid-nineteenth century, the grand parterre was revived in England by designers such as Nesfield and Barry, and fountains were regularly used as the centrepieces.

The parterre may not be a style which will appeal to a keen plantsman, as the opportunities for growing a large range of plants are few. Its appeal lies instead in the precision of its lines, its contrasts of colour and its relation to the adjoining architecture of the house.

Below: Strictly speaking, parterres are filled with blocks of a single colour. However, an alternative approach is to use them as island beds filled with a mixture of shrubs and perennials. These will give varied colour and interest in summer, and still leave you with an ornamental pattern of hedges in winter. The garden will have two distinct identities, the one abundant, the other linear.

Left: Part of the attraction of a parterre is the wide variety of surfaces that can be combined with the structural planting and the different effects that can thereby be achieved. Paths can be gravel – discreet or highly coloured – or paved, as here, or even of grass. The object is to make a pleasing pattern with whichever materials you select.

Above: Plain blocks of colour help to emphasize the shapes and structure of a parterre and to draw attention to the overall pattern by the way colours are repeated. The choice of colours is endless, from subtle pastel shades or single-colour schemes to outrageously bright contrasts. All can be made to work in different, appropriate situations.

A parterre will complement even the most modern of houses because it is a pure geometric design. The modern style of heather-and-conifer garden of the last twenty years is simply a form of arabesque parterre.

A parterre needs to be kept separate from the hurly-burly of a mixed flower garden so that its lines can be appreciated without distraction. An encircling hedge is often all that is required to do this. The Victorians loved to use a grand balustrade to mark the perimeter. With a hedge all round it, a small parterre garden could be made a part of a much larger garden at some distance from the house, but the symmetrical facade of a house is undoubtedly the best backdrop for this sophisticated style of gardening.

Dwarf box is the traditional hedging material for parterres, but yew, cotton lavender, berberis, germander and lavender can all be used. There is no reason at all to be limited to a traditional range of plants, either for hedging or for in-filling. The spaces between hedges could even be filled with water or pebbles instead of the usual bedding plants or bulbs. The same opportunities are offered in the use of modern hard-landscaping materials, producing a wealth of detail in the surface of the paths in a small-scale parterre. Modern sculpture or a modern fountain can be used instead of topiary specimens. Parterres are an unashamed contrivance, to be enjoyed for their bold structure and artistry.

Left: In this modern knot garden the gravel background has been kept deliberately simple to emphasize the pattern of the box hedging.

Below left: Part of the pleasure of a parterre is to be able to walk among the beds, making your own patterns as you cross. A parterre that has no central axis has the appeal of an open-ended maze.

Right: This parterre, in the Victorian manner, has typical vibrantly coloured spring bedding that will be changed again before summer. There is a lot of work in maintaining grass paths but, in a garden of this size, gravel might seem very stark. The huge vase centrepiece could be replaced by topiary, a traditional ornament of parterre gardens.

Below: Vegetables and herbs do not have to be grown in straight rows. They can be surprisingly ornamental in a parterre, and access for picking could not be easier.

Japanese

Japanese gardens have throughout history set out to provide a tranquil environment around the house. They possess an aura of calm which is rarely matched in western garden styles, and almost every element in their composition is symbolic of some aspect of nature or human life. Today the symbolism is not so strong and many gardens in Japan tend to use these symbolic elements for traditional and aesthetic reasons rather than for their meaning. For a westerner, perhaps the best approach to Japanese gardens is to draw from

them the means of arriving at that special stillness and to use it like any other garden tool, instead of trying to produce faithful copies in a foreign land.

Much of that tranquillity derives from an economical, almost minimal use of materials. Each element, whether built or planted, seems heavy upon the ground and settled there. Even water is still or flows gently downwards; you do not find fountains in Japanese gardens. The garden is designed to give the impression of the natural landscape at its most serene. The man-made geometry of some western garden styles is abhorrent to the Japanese.

It is precisely because Japanese gardens discreetly suggest nature, instead of copying it, that they can be created in a space of any size, however small. (At its most extreme, this becomes the miniature landscapes of bonsai.) Western gardeners can learn much from this clever use of small spaces.

The key elements involved are stone, water and a wealth of greenery, arranged in asymmetrical but well-balanced configurations. Flowers, such as irises,

Left: A true Japanese garden is calm and discreet, full of light and shade and contrasts of hard and soft. The paths are gentle and indirect and there is minimal planting.

Far left: Restful Far Eastern gardening can be a wonderful source of inspiration, even when there is no intention to fully reproduce the style in a Western garden.

peonies, lilies and chrysanthemums, play a relatively unimportant part. Groups of stones or boulders can be used to represent mountains and evergreens are clipped to depict boulders, while flat stones may form a gently weaving path. Straight lines are avoided. Water will be present, either as a waterfall, a pool with islands or simply suggested by flowing white sand. Commonly used plants include trees such as plums, cherries and maples and bamboo. Coniferous trees such as pines and juniper are often clipped to form floating cloud shapes, or they can be encouraged to take on a weatherworn appearance. Most significantly, all these plants are used sparingly and are rarely allowed to rub shoulders with one another.

Fences and screens, of materials such as bamboo or grasses, are more common than walls for dividing the garden. Often a loggia is provided from which to view the garden and a lantern of stone or metal is carefully placed to light the path at night or to offer reflections in the water of a pool.

Essentially, a garden in the Japanese style is intended to offer peace and quiet contemplation to its owner and his or her guests, a designer's garden rather than a plantsman's garden. Restraint is everything, with order, harmony and decorum as the guiding principles behind a scheme.

Above: Waterfalls and watercourses are a major element in Japanese gardens and are intended to suggest high mountain streams. Bridges and stone lanterns are also important, symbols of a safe pathway. The cut-leaved, domed Japanese maple (*Acer palmatum dissectum*) is a popular plant for Western versions of Japanese gardens.

Above and bottom far right:
Japanese gardens contain many traditional elements which can be used to suggest an Oriental style. Water is vital. Favourite plants, such as maples, plums, pines and bamboos, will produce the right flavour, especially when set in a carpet of moss. Low mounding evergreens can be used as a substitute for mosses. It is a style that can be adapted to any size garden, as can be seen here, where a small courtyard and an expansive landscape have been equally well served.

Bottom right and above right:
When there is no real water, an impression of a stream or waves can be created by raked sand or gravel or a bed of small stones. Where there is real or imaginary water there are stepping stones; here, wood, stone and foliage combine to present a crisp, clean effect.

Above far right: Bamboo is commonly used to make screens and bridges and well constructed features like this example would be an asset to any Japanese-style garden. Stone lanterns of traditional design are an emphatic Japanese statement.

Classical

In all art forms the classical style is one in which a logical, well-considered form is used as the structure upon which to hang the individual expression of the artist – and so it is with gardens. A classical garden is one which has a structure designed to be pleasing in itself, rather than the largely functional layout of the traditional cottage garden. Within that structure, the planting may be as unrestrained and romantic as you wish, but it will always be seen in relation to the structure of the garden as a whole.

It is no surprise to find that most of the formal period styles of gardening have come under the heading of classical gardens, and there is no denying that symmetry and formality lend a garden the strongest of structures. However, the planting can be vibrantly colourful and extravagant or contained, minimal and quiet. This is the great advantage of a classical garden: its good bones will support all manner of fleshing out.

Throughout history it has been the classical gardens which have survived, from the green simplicity of an eighteenth-century landscape park with its lakes and temples to the geometric razzmatazz of Baroque gardens. But the twentieth century has seen the development of classical gardens on a much smaller scale, where the blend of domestic architecture and plantsman's gardening have complemented each other perfectly. English gardens like Sissinghurst

Below: Classical gardens have strong bones – a clear and attractive structure which can then be enriched by planting. Light and shade and the qualities given to a design by the inclusion of water are almost more important than the overlay of planting, which need not be colourful.

Left: Symmetry plays an important role in classical gardens, repetition of parts being the easiest way of producing balanced arrangements that are strong and visually satisfying.

Above: The formal structure of a classical garden, frequently composed of walls, hedges, paving and sculpture, should be coupled with a sympathetic, complementary selection of plants.

(designed by Vita Sackville-West and Sir Harold Nicolson) and Great Dixter (by Sir Edwin Lutyens) and Dumbarton Oaks (by Beatrix Farrand) in the United States have proved that gardens rich in architectural and structural detail will happily support the most exuberant of planting and win the affections of all serious gardeners. In gardens like these, form and content reach a most satisfactory balance, which surely is the essence of a classical garden.

A well-designed garden deserves to be well planted, and when making a classical garden it is worth planting carefully with an eye for shape, colour and texture. The plants may form part of the structure itself, in hedges or recurring patterns of specimen plants. Water, either standing, running or as a fountain may form part of the design. Even within a small garden it is possible to make use of vistas and focal points, while ensuring that the open spaces intended to be part of the design do not fall prey to a clutter of specimen plants. It is too easy to let the planting obscure rather than enhance the design.

Well-built walls, doorways, arches, steps, paths and pergolas will all enhance the quality of the garden structure, and occasionally a good-sized urn or vase will add distinction. So will an attractive garden bench carefully placed. Good quality hard landscaping can be expensive, but it is undoubtedly the key to success when making a classical garden. Few great gardens, however, were made in a season, but were built up gradually over the years. This is the best way to approach your own plans for a classical garden.

Left: Classical gardens, in relying on a strong structure and plan, tend to use a good deal of hard landscaping, often of antique appearance.

Right: Period features such as parterres can be introduced into classical gardens. The twentieth-century idea of separate "garden rooms" fits in well with the classical tradition, allowing different planting styles to be used within the various sections of the overall design.

Bottom right: Simplicity of structure is one of the keynotes of classical gardens. The emphasis here is linear.

Below: High quality materials skilfully combined with simple planting, as here, will always produce a classical garden.

Subtropical

The so-called subtropical garden is really a trick. We are used to seeing in our gardens plants from all over the world, from the most extravagant rhododendron to the most delicate alpine primula; but usually these plants come from a climate broadly similar to our own. In the subtropical garden, the aim is to present a picture of a totally different climate in which the usual range of temperate plants will not grow. To do this is inevitably a deception, but a satisfying one.

The subtropical style of gardening involves using a range of plants which might seem more at home in a much hotter climate, although they must of course be able to grow in our own gardens. It is achieved by selecting those plants with the most appropriate foliage; but perhaps more importantly, it is achieved by avoiding those plants which are commonplace in temperate gardens. The absence of certain plants is just as telling as the choice of plants used.

By the same token, subtropical gardens are often best sited in an enclosed area where the presence of the temperate world outside cannot dilute the effect you are trying to achieve. The same goes for garden architecture, furniture and hard landscaping. It is better to avoid the hallmarks of other garden styles such as classical urns and familiar, traditional garden seats and paving techniques. Instead, try to keep hard surfaces as informal as possible. Gravel is the most discreet option but clay tiles are another possibility. Stay with unsophisticated materials wherever possible. Cane or bamboo seats will look right.

Water can be important in creating a subtropical garden. If you want to give the impression of a hot dry climate, then a pool or a fountain is ideal. If the aim is

Left: The great paddle-shaped leaves of cannas always look suitably exotic, especially those forms with bronzed foliage. Although in temperate parts of the world cannas are grown mainly for their impressive leaves, their large flowers can produce a brilliant tropical effect, coming in bold shades of red, orange and deep pink, taking complex forms.

to reproduce a jungle effect, running, trickling or dripping water may be more appropriate, with moss and ferns growing alongside to enhance the effect.

Subtropical climates tend to produce large, lush foliage and this should be imitated in your choice of plants. The paddle-shaped banana leaf is to be found in cannas and lysichitums; spiky rosettes are found in yuccas, cordylines and potted agaves; araucarias can be useful too. For sheer size of leaf, there is no beating the Chusan palm, *Trachycarpus fortunei*, and paulownia and ailanthus trees can be stooled to produce huge leaves. Gunnera and *Rheum palmatum* both produce huge herbaceous leaves in damp soil and in similar conditions bamboos and phormium can be used to give an exotic touch. In dryer conditions, *Melianthus major* offers lush blue-grey foliage. Climbers such as passion flowers, gourds and menispermum can add a tangled, jungle flavour, and daturas in pots will provide wonderfully exotic trumpet flowers rather like a hibiscus. In general, however, foliage is a better tool than flowers in creating the effect of an alien climate: it can offer the promise of subtropical flowers without ever giving the game away.

In some climates it is necessary to create the subtropical effect under glass or at least partial cover, where the higher temperatures and reduced winds will better suit many large-leaved plants.

Far left: As long as plants look exotic and foreign, they can be used, no matter how many continents the result actually represents. The jungle effect is enhanced by running water.

Below: The combination of potted aspidistra, Chusan palms and a reflecting pool helps to create an "oasis" look. The palms produce fragrant yellow flowers.

Right: Palm fronds and handsome large leaves are the hallmarks of the colonial-style subtropical garden. Tall, mature palms create the ideal, lush impression.

Below left: Even where the climate is temperate, and especially in coastal gardens, there is scope for using plants that impart an exotic flavour, such as the yuccas flanking these steps. Simple touches like this, combined with the use of suitable hard landscaping materials, can make all the difference to a design. Such strategic use of plants and features is a device that will serve any garden style; one ideal element can crown the effect.

Below right: Given overhead cover, you can grow a wide range of large-leaved plants, both hardy and not-so-hardy, which in the open would not look as lush and exotic because of the wind and the drier atmosphere. *Rodgersia podophylla* (as underplanting in the centre) is perfectly hardy in an open space, but looks and is at home in the cool, moist shade beneath taller foliage plants.

Right: In a hot, dry climate the sound of trickling water from a fountain is always welcome. It is a reminder of fresh peacefulness in the oppressive heat of the day. The sound of a stream smacks much more of greyer, cooler climates with plentiful rain, so it is less appropriate to a subtropical garden.

Above right: The dry heat of central America and Africa can be simulated by the use of succulents and cacti. Where soil would be expected to look dry, gravel or pebbles can be successfully used as ground cover. Select light shades of stones and other surfaces to suggest arid conditions.

Roof Gardens and Terraces

Roof gardens and terraces are both conceived as extensions to the buildings to which they are attached rather than being part of wider garden schemes. The added attraction of a roof garden is, of course, its view. There may not be much choice as to siting (for the one sits above the house and the other alongside it), but most roof gardens and terraces have sun for a good part of the day and can be made shady and sheltered where necessary with overhead supports for scented climbers.

There can be no more ingenious use of space in terms of garden design than roof gardens, but these

features should not be undertaken lightly. Even modest rooftop plans should be checked with a structural engineer or architect who will be able to determine the load-bearing capacity of the roof, for the weight of hard landscaping, growing mediums (especially when wet) and plants can be considerable. Moving materials to the top of buildings can also be tiring and time-consuming. Whether you decide upon just a few tubs full of plants of a full-blown rooftop garden, however, the result should be well worth the effort.

Terraces also involve a certain amount of construction work, especially if the area around the house needs levelling. Solid foundations are also important in order to bear the weight of people, plants and furniture.

Care must be taken over the type of flooring used for roof gardens and terraces. Grass is obviously a non-starter (apart from astroturf, which can be cut and laid like carpet), and alternatives range from stone and brick (for terraces only), to timber decking,

Far left: This densely planted roof garden makes use of a sturdy, firmly fixed trellis covered with hardy climbers to provide privacy and protection against the wind.

Left: This trellised archway is both decorative and practical, providing shade, a windbreak and dividing up the roof space into different areas.

Below: This extensive brick terrace is surrounded by gently sloping banks of shrubs and plant-filled containers. The angle at which the bricks are set creates a strong directional pull towards the steps. This tempts the onlooker to explore another hidden area of the garden, having surveyed the scene from the wooden bench.

suitable for both roofs and terraces. It is very important that flooring should be non-slip in both contexts and that drainage is efficient and well maintained.

In creating these self-contained areas, privacy is a main consideration. Banks of plant-filled containers of varying sizes can be positioned to shield the outside world, or a trellis covered with climbers can be used

for a more permanent effect. As roof gardens are often exposed to the wind, screening is also a practical way of creating shelter from wind eddies, although they must be securely fixed to the house, as should containers and other planters. Having created an outside "room", garden furniture can be introduced.

As for planting, both roof gardens and terraces rely heavily on frequent seasonal changes provided mostly by containers and raised beds, with perhaps a solid background of good reliable shrubs to give a sense of continuity. Fragrance should be considered as an important characteristic, especially with *al fresco* dining. Summer-flowering jasmine, lilies in tubs, night-scented stock (which is so quickly and easily grown from a pinch of seed) and nicotianas are all deliciously perfumed and, for the rest of the year, shrubby herbs like thyme, rosemary and sage will release their scent when lightly brushed or crushed. These are ideal plants for raised beds.

Far left: The floor of this roof garden consists of different levels of timber decking. The planks have been laid at right angles to create areas of contrasting shapes within a rather regular L-shaped layout. Silvery-grey shrubs and half-hardy annuals combine in a fragrant, low-maintenance planting scheme.

Left: Although rather unsophisticated, this mix of bright colours creates a lively, informal feel. Small pots like these need watering at least once a day, with regular feeding and dead-heading.

Below left: For a colourful springtime terrace display, flowering bulbs like these tulips are ideal. The simple terracotta containers can be replanted throughout the year to provide constant seasonal interest, although the well-clipped box will provide year-round appeal. However, if very cold weather does threaten then all the pots should be moved indoors so they do not suffer fractures caused by frost damage.

Above: As well as plant material, terraces can be ornamented with a variety of garden accessories. These can range from the functional, as in the case of tables and chairs, to the aesthetic, for example, planters and decorative containers. Here, a pair of matching pots on either side of the steps add an air of formality to this raised area and frame the bench, which has been placed against a sheltering wall.

Left: The complex paving patterns and attractive formal trelliswork dominate this terrace scheme. For this reason, the planting has been kept relatively unambitious, with sparse but effective groups of containers creating areas of impact. The lilies and large foliage subjects have been chosen for their simplicity, while wall plants soften the perimeter boundary but preserve the uncluttered, spacious feel.

Container

Never let it be said that container gardens are second best to gardens in the soil. They may be labour-intensive, but, as a reward, they can be as rich and extravagant as your pocket and patience will allow.

Containers solve many problems for would-be gardeners. They are the answer for a paved town courtyard and a roof terrace ten storeys high, and an excellent solution for people who cannot bend easily to dig. They are an ideal finishing touch: an array of window boxes can complete a house front. Whatever the reason, the choice of containers is enormous.

However, certain ground rules need to be borne in mind. You need to consider the work involved in occasional changes of soil and the ease of access; most important of all, you need to consider watering. Do

Above: Pelargoniums provide a bright summer display in this formal garden. Pots of flowers are set into permanent containers allowing for change during the season. The empty pots provide winter ornament.

Right: Potted citrus trees are a feature of Italian gardens. The orangeries of English historic gardens were built to overwinter such trees which were then displayed outdoors during the summer.

the containers have adequate drainage? Is there a water supply nearby? Will you be able to use liquid feeds? What will happen if you are away for a weekend or on holiday? Watering is by far the greatest chore of container gardening and it needs to be done generously and regularly. Rain is never adequate on its own and can fool you into thinking the containers are wetter then they really are. Automatic irrigation is well worth considering for a large container garden.

Below: Alpines are the perfect plants for stone or imitation stone troughs. Although most of these plants need perfect drainage they will still need watering in dry weather.

It is important to decide whether to plant for a 12-month display or to let the containers remain empty during the winter. Remember that many plants which would be hardy enough in the ground may succumb to the cold when their roots are raised up in a container open to frosts. Frozen, waterlogged soil can also burst containers as it expands. Conversely, containers in sun can get very hot in summer and your choice of plants needs to be governed by this fact: it is all too easy to bake the roots of plants.

With these practical points in mind, you are free to choose from the gamut of container gardening styles. Formal courtyards can be graced with potted bays, sentinel cypresses, camellias or bamboos. In addition, some especially beautiful pots may look best not

planted but used as an architectural contrast. Large concrete planters can be filled with trees and shrubs, almost as if they were in the ground. Stone troughs can be planted as miniature gardens of alpines or screes, but they can equally be filled with a single carpeting plant as a piece of living sculpture.

In a more cottagey style, tubs, pots and even baskets of all shapes and sizes can be clustered to form splashes of colour, by doorways or lining steps. Window boxes and hanging baskets blend in well with this style and provide an opportunity for bold or restful incidental planting in prime locations.

With the aid of a circulating pump, even water can be a feature of container gardens, either as a small fountain or trickling over pebbles from one container to another. Certainly such details add great charm.

Right and below: Container gardening need not be formal. A glorious clutter of interesting, well-filled pots can look splendid and can give a Mediterranean air to your garden. Only remember that every pot you use is another one to water. Hanging baskets are the hardest of all to keep moist. All sorts of containers make interesting planters so there is no need to stick to commercially available ones, as long as you remember to provide drainage holes. Copper wash-tubs or polythene-lined baskets make attractive tubs, and bought pots can be painted and decorated to suit the style of your garden.

Bottom: An arrangement of containers that is loosely symmetrical is a very appealing way of arranging a busy mixture of pots and harmonious plants.

Opposite, top and bottom left: A rigidly formal arrangement of containers is a useful way of accentuating strong, adjoining architectural features.

Opposite, bottom right: Pots and troughs, when well placed, are a form of sculpture in themselves. The effect is enhanced here by simple, single-species planting. The row of tulip-filled containers is sited to echo the curve of the parterre behind.

Acid A term applied to soil or water with a pH value of below 7.

Alkaline A term applied to soil or water with a pH value of above 7.

Annual A plant that completes its life cycle within one growing season.

Calcareous Containing, or resembling, carbonate of lime or limestone; chalky or limy in nature.

Compost (seed or potting) A mixture of materials consisting chiefly of loam, peat, sand and fertilizers. It is used as a medium for sowing seeds, planting on seedlings and potting plants.

Coniferous Relating to the group of plants that typically bear cones. Most of these are evergreen and have linear leaves.

Container-grown A plant in a container as opposed to a bare-rooted one that is lifted from the open ground.

Cultivar A cultivated, as distinct from a botanical, variety of plant.

Cutting A separated piece of stem, root or leaf taken from a plant in order to propagate a new plant.

Deadhead To cut off a wilting or faded flower head from a plant.

Deciduous A plant that loses all its leaves at one time of the year, usually during late autumn.

Desiccating wind A wind that dries plants, soil and organic material.

Division A method of propagation by means of dividing a single plant into smaller portions; also a way of thinning plants.

Dormancy The resting period of a plant, usually over winter.

Double (flower) A flower with a double row or multiple rows of petals.

Dressing A top covering, like pea gravel, applied to the surface of the soil.

Ericaceous Species of plant belonging to the heather family, Ericaceae, which includes azaleas and rhododendrons. Most will not grow in limy soil.

Evergreen The term given to a plant that retains its leaves throughout the year; opposite to deciduous.

Germination The term given to the development of a seed into a seedling.

Glaucous A bluish-white, bluish-green and bluish-grey waxy bloom.

Habit The natural mode of growth and consequent shape of a plant.

Half-hardy A plant that is unable to survive the prevailing winter temperatures without some sort of protection, but one that does not need to be kept in a greenhouse all the year round.

Harden off To acclimatize plants that are raised in warm conditions to cooler conditions.

Hard landscaping The main constituents of a garden's design and construction, referring to items such as walling and paving.

Hardy A plant capable of surviving the winter in the open without protection.

Herbaceous A non-woody, fleshy plant grown in borders; usually a perennial.

Humus Fertile, partially decomposed organic matter in soil.

Hybrid A plant that is produced by the cross-fertilization of two species or variants of species.

Inorganic The use of artificial chemicals in the garden.

Knot garden A formal garden of ornamental flower beds, planted with low-growing plants and hedges, that are arranged in an intricate, twisted design.

Layering A method of propagation in which a shoot or stem is induced to form roots while still attached to the parent plant.

Leafmould A type of organic matter consisting of decayed leaves used to enrich the soil.

Loam Any reasonably fertile soil that contains a free-draining mixture of clay, sand and organic material.

Microclimate A climate particular to a specific situation which differs from the overall climate of the garden or region.

Mulch A soil-covering that protects plants, reduces evaporation, suppresses weeds, prevents erosion and, in the case of organic mulch, enriches the soil.

Organic Gardening without using artificial chemicals.

Parterre A formal garden made up of elaborately shaped flower beds designed to be viewed from above.

Perennial A plant that lives for at least three seasons.

pH The scale by which acidity or alkalinity is measured; a pH value of below 7 is acid and above 7 is alkaline.

Photosynthesis The process by which a green plant makes carbohydrates from water and carbon dioxide (with the release of oxygen) using light and chlorophyll.

Pleaching A technique for forming a dense hedge by interweaving the branches of well-spaced plants, usually trees such as limes or hornbeams, and often leaving bare trunks as stilts.

Potager The term given to a decorative or ornamental kitchen garden.

Propagation The production of a new plant from an existing one, either sexually by seed or asexually by cuttings.

Rhizome An underground stem, sometimes thick as in irises and other times thin as in grasses, and usually growing horizontally.

Rootstock The underground part of a plant from which roots and shoots grow.

Seedling A very young plant with just a few leaves, raised from seed.

Semi-evergreen Describes a plant intermediate between evergreen and deciduous. It bears some foliage throughout the year, but also loses some leaves during winter.

Single (flower) A flower with a single layer of petals.

Soft landscaping The main constituents of a garden's design and construction, referring only to planting and turfing.

Species The term given to a group of closely related oranisms within a genus.

Spike (flower) An inflorescence consisting of stalkless flowers arranged along a stem.

Stooling To cut to the ground periodically and allow to regrow in order to encourage the growth of new whip-like stems.

Sub-shrub A type of plant which has a woody base and herbaceous tips.

Subsoil The term given to the layer of soil below the topsoil. It is lighter in colour than the topsoil.

Tamp To pack down a material such as soil or concrete very firmly.

Tender A plant that is unable to withstand the coldest prevailing weather conditions.

Tilth The fine, crumbly surface layer of soil. The ideal tilth for a seedbed is about the same consistency as coarse breadcrumbs.

Topsoil The term given to the upper layer of soil, the darkest and most fertile part, in which plants grow.

Trompe l'oeil A painting or decoration giving a convincing illusion of reality.

Variegated Leaves with attractive white, yellow or pinky markings.

Variety A distinct variant of a species, either a cultivated form (a cultivar) or one that occurs naturally.

Watering in To water around the stem of a newly planted plant to settle the soil.

GARDEN DESIGNERS AND LANDSCAPE ARCHITECTS

Acres Wild (Landscape and Garden Design)
45a High Street
Billingshurst
West Sussex
RH14 9PP

Argyll Landscapes
Drishaig
Inverary
Argyll
PA32 8XQ
Creative gardening and instant trees, all varieties supplied and planted anywhere.

Margaret Bestwick
12 Orchard Lane
Woodnewton
Peterborough
PE8 5EE
Exclusive formal or informal designs. Construction drawings and planting plans drawn up to suit customers' individual requirements.

Jean Bishop & Partner
Wood Farm
Dunston
Norwich
Norfolk
NR14 8QD

Alison Brett Garden Design
18 Dighton Road
Wandsworth
London
SW18 1AN

Chenies Landscape Design
Bramble Lane
London Road
East Amersham
Buckinghamshire
HP7 9DH
Landscape architects for all aspects of landscape design. Chelsea Flower Show gold medal winners.

Helen Clay Garden Design
Lings Cottage
Henson Lane
Cropwell Butler
Nottinghamshire
NG12 2JS

Alison Coleman
17 Kent Close
Bromborough
Wirral
L63 OEF
Trained in graphic design and horticulutre, Alison Coleman combines her skills to offer a complete service in garden design, including visualization and illustration.

Irene George Bsc MA ALI
2 Pollicott Cottages
Ashenden
Buckinghamshire
HP18 OHH
Landscape architect with experience in design of town and country gardens.

Alexander Greenshields
Flat 2a
34 Boxridge Avenue
Purley
Surrey
CR8 3AQ

Duncan Heather
34 Kings Road
Henley-on-Thames
Oxfordshire
RG9 2DG

The Julian Dowle Partnership
The Old Malt House
High Street
Newent
Gloucestershire
GL18 1AY

Landsberg & Newnham Garden Design
4 Campion Road
Putney
London
SW15 6NW
For romantic, zany or formal gardens in the town or country. Services range from consultation to full designs, including site survey and complete working drawings for constructions and planting.

Landsberg and Garden Design Consultants
4 Sandy Lodge Way
Northwood
Middlesex
Professionally qualified landscape architects who specialize in the design and building of town and country gardens; garden planning, planting design, pools, ornamental features, and garden buildings using new or reclaimed materials.

Lees Associates
5 Dryden Street
Covent Garden
London
WC2E 9NW
Landscape architecture. Romantic and traditional garden design.

Frances Traylen Martin Dip. ISD
Saint's Hill House
Penshurst
Tonbridge
Kent
TN11 8EN

Garden designer professionally qualified provides designs for traditional or modern, period or neglected gardens. Full working drawings and planting plans.

Graham A. Pavey & Associates
11 Runces Road
Bromham
Bedfordshire
MK43 8QD

Roland Mayer-Jones BSc (Hons) Hort.
Merlindere
Old Monmouth Road
Longhope
Gloucestershire
GL17 OPD
A professional garden design/consultancy service.

Hugh O'Connell
MSGD
English Garden Designs
100 Yonder Street
Ottery St. Mary
Devon
EX11 1HH
From large country houses to city centre courtyards.

Plantation Group Limited
Temple Gardens
Holloway Lane
Harmondsworth
West Drayton
Middlesex
UB7 OAD
Garden design and landscape gardening, also water features.

Plantech Garden Design
75 Curzon Street
Caln
Wiltshire
SN11 ODW
A comprehensive and professional design service. Re-establishment of old gardens and designs, plus consultancy and soil testing.

Sue Prideaux Garden Design
Selehurst
Lower Beeding
Horsham
Sussex
RH13 6PR

Redman Garden Designs
51 Shandon Road
London
SW4 9HS
Consultancy, garden design, planting and maintenance.

Sally Walker Garden Design
Bowling Alley Cottage
The Green
Horsted Keynes
West Sussex
RH17 7AP

A range of services from consultation through to construction and planting. London and south England.

Sheridans
37 Northcote Road
St. Margarets
Twickenham
Middlesex
TW1 1PB
A range of services including garden design and construction; restoration and reclamation; year-round maintenance. Specialists in oriental gardens, herbaceous plants and uncommon ones.

Squires Landscapes
Holloway Hill
Chertsey
Surrey
KT16 OAE

Andrew Stansfield
188 Station Road
Harpenden
Hertfordshire
AL5 4UL
Works as a garden designer, landscape architect and horticulturist.

Joanna Stay
67 Dalton Street
St. Albans
Hertfordshire
AL3 5QH
Professionally qualified in garden design, horticulture and M.S.G.D. Advisory visits, designs and full working drawings offered.

Jacqui Stubbs Associates
24 Duncan Road
Richmond
Surrey
TW9 2JD
Design service provided for large and small gardens alike. Services range from half day consultations to full design surveys and planting plans. Brochure available on request.

Town and Country Gardens
8 Willow Walk
Petworth
Sussex
GU28 OEY
An established garden construction company well known for its high-quality workmanship. Specializes in individual designs.

Stephen John White
12 Witt Road
Fair Oak
Eastleigh
Hampshire
SO5 7FR

ACKNOWLEDGEMENTS

Sue Atkinson 74 bottom left/Mitchell Beazley 8, 15, 34, 38, 40, 42 top left, top right and bottom, 46, 47 bottom, 49 bottom, 50 left, 51 bottom left, 53 bottom right, 56 top, 57 top, 59 top right, 60 left, 62 left, 63 right, 65 bottom, 66, 67 top right, bottom left and right, 71 top right, 76 left, 77 right, 78 top, bottom left and bottom right, 79 bottom left, 80-81, 82 top right and bottom left, 82-83, 88 left, 88-89, 89 right, 90 bottom right, 91 top right, 96 left, 96-97, 100-101, 104 left, 108-109, 110 top, 111 top, 112 left, 114 bottom left and bottom right

Stephen Anderton 101 right, 111 bottom

Paul Barker/Mitchell Beazley 11 top, 16, 41 top, centre and bottom, 43 bottom, 47 top left, 48, 53 top left and bottom left, 56-57 bottom, 58 bottom left, 60-61 bottom, 62 top, 62-63 bottom, 63 top, 65 top left and top right, 67 top left, 76-77, 79 top, 81 top right and bottom right, 83 bottom right, 90 bottom left, 90-91, 91 right of centre, bottom left and bottom right, 100 left, 109 right, 121

Tommy Candler 103 top

Eric Crichton 10 bottom, 44 left and right, 47 top right, 49 top, 51 top and bottom right, 56 bottom left, 58-59 top, 61 right, 64, 70 top and bottom, 74 top left, 75 bottom left, 82 top left, 86 bottom, 87 top right, 98 top and bottom left, 99 right of centre, 105 right, 106 bottom left, 107 top and bottom, 100 top right

Garden Picture Library/Tim Griffiths 117 right, /Jerry Pavia 94 top left and bottom, /JS Sira 119 top, /Ron Sutherland 71 top left, 73 right, 87 bottom (D: Duane Paul Design Team), /Brigitte Thomas 72 left

John Glover 11 bottom, 13, 21 bottom, 31 top, 118 top left (D: Anthony Paul Design Team)

Jerry Harpur 9, 21 top, 32-33 (D: Claus Scheinert, Alpes Maritimes), 36 top left and bottom (D: Claus Scheinert, Alpes Maritimes), 37 (D: Claus Scheinert, Alpes Maritimes), 39 top (D: Claus Scheinert, Alpes Maritimes), 39 bottom, 45 bottom (D: Claus Scheinert, Alpes Maritimes), 58-59 bottom (D: Susie Ranicar, Tasmania), 71 bottom

(Meadowbrook Farm, Philadelphia), 84 left (D: Judith Sharpe), 86 top, 92 left (D: Polly Park, Canberra, Australia), 92-93 (D: Patrick Miller, San Francisco), 93 right (D: Gary Orr, San Francisco), 94 right (D: Keyes Landscape, Camden, London), 95 top (D: Garrett Eckbo, San Francisco), 99 top (D: Bruce Kelly, New York), 104-5 (Japanese Stroll Garden, Long Island), 106 top left (D: John Patrick, Melbourne, Victoria), 112-113, 114-115, 116-117, 118 top right (D: Sonny Garcia, San Francisco), 122 top left (D: Ann Alexander-Sinclair), 123 top and bottom right (D: Edwina von Gal, New York)

John Heseltine 95 bottom left

Marijke Heuff 79 bottom right, 83 top left, 99 bottom, 102 top and bottom, 106 top right

Michele Lamontagne 72-73

Andrew Lawson 12, 17, 18, 50 right, 54 top right, 74-75, 87 top left, 119 bottom

Georges Leveque/Dominique Lafourcade 20

Clive Nichols title page (D: Anthony Noel), 22 (D: Sue Guerney), 23, 30, 31 bottom, 35 top, 52, 53 top right, 54 top left and bottom, 55 bottom, 68-69, 84-85 (23 Beechcroft Road, Oxford), 85 right (D: Anthony Noel), 98 bottom right, 103 bottom, 115 top right, 118 bottom (D: Sue Guerney), 120 left, 122 bottom

Hugh Palmer 10 top, 19, 45 top, 60-61 top, 83 top right, 95 bottom right, 97 right, 110 bottom, 113 right, 115 bottom right, 116 left, 120-121, 123 bottom left

Brigitte and Philippe Perdereau half title, 14 /Thomas 55 top

Photos Horticultural 59 bottom right

Reed Consumer Books Picture Library/W.F. Davidson 108 left, /Jerry Harpur 43 top, /George Wright 35 bottom, 57 and 75 bottom right